Things to Make for Children

By the Editors of Sunset Books and Sunset Magazine

Lane Publishing Co. • Menlo Park, California

Foreword

A sure way of delighting a child is to give him a toy. And if you make the plaything yourself, its value to the child is all the greater (as is your satisfaction in giving it). This book is a complete revision of the first edition of *Things to Make for Children,* published in 1960. It contains a large selection of playthings that an adult can make for a child. The projects range from wooden cars and rag dolls to play yard equipment and party ideas. You'll find educational playthings, toys that stimulate creativity, ideas for both outdoor play and quiet indoor activities, and toys designed purely for fun. Many doll houses and ideas for decorating and furnishing children's rooms are also included.

The materials required for all of the projects are commonly available in hardware stores, lumber yards, fabric stores, or craft and hobby shops. No specialized techniques or methods are required for making any of the projects. You can follow the illustrated instructions provided for each or modify them to best suit your child.

When making any of the projects, be sure to keep safety in mind. Make the toys strong enough to withstand wear and tear. Try to avoid small parts that could easily break off, and be especially careful when assembling a toy with nails that would be dangerously exposed if the toy broke. To avoid sharp edges and splinters on wooden toys, sand all of their surfaces. Use only nontoxic paint and finishes to decorate toys.

Two companion Sunset books that you might enjoy are *Children's Rooms and Play Yards,* containing ideas for furnishing children's rooms and equipping play yards, and *Crafts for Children,* presenting craft ideas and hobbies for children themselves to pursue.

Edited by Richard Osborne

Design: Michael A. Rogondino

Illustrations: Joe Seney

Cover Photograph: Lars Speyer

Editor, Sunset Books: David E. Clark

Sixth Printing October 1977

Library of Congress No. 73-75756. ISBN Title No. 0-376-04703-8.

Lithographed in the United States.

Contents

SEE FACING PAGE FOR INSTRUCTIONS

4 SMALL WOODEN TOYS

Small Wooden Toys

Trucks and Cars

Toy cars and trucks are always favorites of children. Here are some that can be made easily from inexpensive materials.

   All of the vehicles here were cut from 4 by 6 Douglas fir on a band saw. A band saw is the best tool to use on wood this size, but a jigsaw, coping saw, sabre saw, or even a keyhole saw will work if the size of the toys is scaled down to match the tools. You might find it easier to cut two 2 by 4s separately to the shape of the toy and then cement them together.

   Whether you copy the silhouettes shown here or design your own cars, it is best to keep the shapes simple. Avoid creating sharp corners whenever possible. Sharp corners that are necessary should be sanded smooth to make the toys safest.

   Start making the cars by drawing the shapes onto the wood, and then cutting them out. Cut out the windows with a $3/4$ or 1-inch drill bit on either a drill press or hand drill. Sand the edges of the holes to prevent splinters and cracking.

   The wheels are made from $1\frac{3}{4}$-inch doweling. After they are cut and sanded, drill a $1/4$-inch hole, $1/4$ inch into the center of each wheel. Drill two $5/16$-inch holes through the body of the car and use $1/4$-inch dowels, long enough to go through the car body and be cemented to the wheels, for the axles. Leave the toys unfinished or treat them with nontoxic paint.

SIMPLE CARS AND TRUCKS (above, facing page) captivate children's fancy. Their varied shapes (below) can be cut from 4 by 6 blocks of fir on a band saw (below, left) or from 2 by 4s. Rough profile, penciled on wood, helps guide the saw.

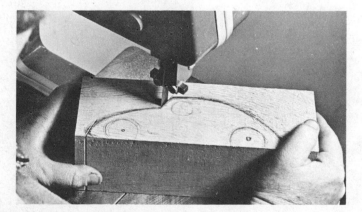

Wooden Boats

Freighters, tankers, tugs, and yachts will keep a young admiral busy in the bathtub or on the living room floor, and are easy to make. The materials include pieces of 1 by 3, 1 by 4, and 2 by 4 pine or fir and pieces of dowel.

To make each boat, just cut one piece of wood into the shape of the hull, and then cement other pieces onto it to form cabins, smokestacks, and masts. Be sure to sand all corners and edges so they will be smooth and rounded. Leave the wood natural or finish it with nontoxic paint.

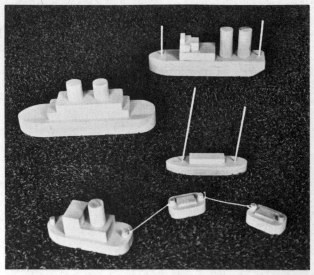

BUDDING YOUNG ADMIRALS will enjoy a fleet of wooden ships, made by cutting scraps of wood and gluing them together. For boats that float use light wood: fir or pine.

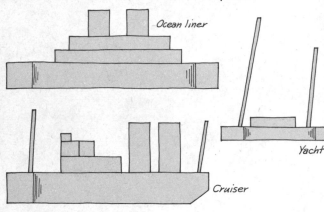

Ocean liner

Cruiser

Yacht

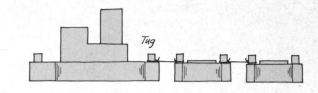

Tug

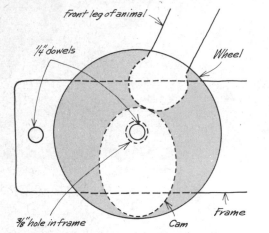

front leg of animal

¼" dowels

Wheel

⅜" hole in frame

Cam

Frame

BOBBING ANIMALS — horse (below) and bird (below right) — are pull toys. Triple exposure of bird shows bobbing motion. Art (above) shows construction.

Cam Critters

Wooden pull toys that bob up and down have always amused young children. The animals shown here can be cut out of 1-inch softwood on a jigsaw. The frame consists of two pieces of 1 by 2-inch wood secured about 1 inch apart with a length of ¼-inch dowel at each end. The wheels are also cut from 1-inch softwood and are fixed onto ¼-inch dowel axles that pass through ⅜-inch holes in the frame members.

The toys' bobbing motion is due to an elliptical cam, fixed off center on the front axle between the two frame pieces. The animal's front portion rests on the cam and moves up and down as the wheels turn. The animal pivots on the rear axle, which passes through a ⅜-inch hole drilled through the animal's hind portion.

Whimsical Wobble Toys

These whimsical toys, made at home from odds and ends, come to life in the hands of a child. As they are pushed or pulled about, a mother hen feeds her young, flowers grow, and a snake charmer and his hypnotized snake weave from side to side.

In each case the motion comes from one of two basic mechanical systems employing special cams: one makes the toy bob up and down; the other produces a swaying from side to side. Details are shown in the sketches.

For ease of operation, make the moving parts out of a light wood such as fir or pine. The base should be made from a heavier wood, perhaps oak or walnut, to provide stability.

All the dowels are either ½ or ¼ inch in diameter. The dowels should fit snugly in the drilled holes, so that you can assemble the toy "dry" and make final adjustments of the moving parts before using glue to make the connections permanent. You will have to experiment to get the two parts of the double cam separated enough so they work without binding or slipping.

The raw materials used to make these toys range from scraps left over from a patio roof to a stray sink strainer and pipe cleaners and they might suggest others that you could find around the house or at a hobby or hardware store. The wheels are 2-inch drawer pulls mounted on ¼-inch dowel axles. The mother hen and her chicks were cut from small pieces of pine; she feeds the children a pipe cleaner worm. The gardener wears a sliding door pull for his hat; the snake charmer's turban is a porcelain closet cap. Torsos for the gardener and snake charmer are wooden sock darners with the handles removed; one of the leftover handles was used for the snake. Wooden beads of various sizes can be used for heads, hands, and feet.

Paint the toys according to your fancy with nontoxic paint and finally rub a bar of soap along all the friction points, particularly around the edges of the cams. This "lubrication" will make the toys operate without binding or sticking. The four-wheel toys are pulled by a string, the two-wheelers by a length of dowel rigidly attached to the body.

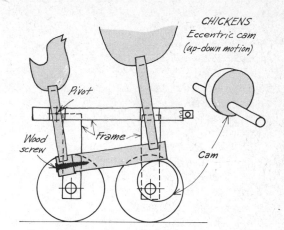

CHICKENS
Eccentric cam
(up-down motion)

Pivot

Frame

Wood screw

Cam

Moving parts, except wheels & axles, shown in tone

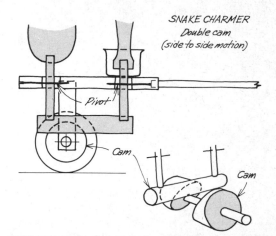

SNAKE CHARMER
Double cam
(side to side motion)

Pivot

Cam

Cam

Cam

PUSH-PULL TOYS (below) bob up and down or wobble from side to side. For bobbing motion, set a section of dowel off center on axle (top drawing). Wobble is produced by a 1½-inch length of dowel cut at a 30° angle and fixed to the axle (bottom drawing).

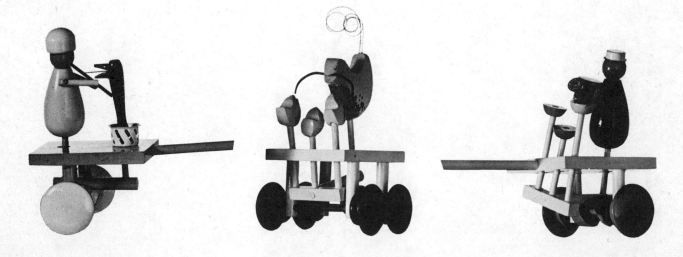

Plywood Shapes for a Zoo

Little more than assorted pieces of thin plywood, these delightful, inexpensive toys will give a child hours of fun as he creates figures and animals with them.

The toys consist of bodies made by sandwiching three pieces of plywood together as shown in the photograph. (White glue or all-purpose cement can be used for this.) Single pieces then slip into the sandwich to create various forms. Blocks of wood with grooves cut into their surfaces hold the finished forms upright.

For the bodies and single pieces, get 1/8-inch-thick lauan plywood (called "door-skin" at lumber yards). A 3 by 6-foot sheet of plywood will give you about twice as many pieces as were used to make the toys in the photograph.

You'll also need a 4-foot length of 1 by 3 lumber for the bases. Cut a 1/2-inch-deep slot lengthwise down the middle of this board with a circular saw (most small circular-saw blades make 1/8-inch-wide slots that will fit the plywood legs). If you don't have access to a circular saw, a lumber yard can cut this slot. Saw off sections of any length for the bases.

Cut whatever shapes you like for the single pieces and bodies. You might try circles, ellipses, triangles, rectangles, teardrops, trapezoids, and quarter and half moons. Just remember that you'll need two pieces of the same shape for each body sandwich. Make the center piece of each sandwich small enough to leave a 3/4-inch-deep slot on all sides. After you glue a body sandwich together, lay it on a flat surface and place a weight on it so the parts will be squeezed together while they dry.

The finish on the toys shown here is orange shellac, which dries quickly and helps the pieces stick together. Instead of shellac, you might use stain, varnish, or nontoxic paint. The easiest way of finishing the toys is to treat the entire sheet of plywood before cutting it into different shapes. If you want more than one color, cut the sheet into medium-sized sections—one for each color. Single body pieces that fit loosely can be given a second coat of finish to make them fit more snugly.

ANIMAL PARTS are simply various shapes cut from plywood. Each body and head consists of three pieces sandwiched together with white glue (top). To assemble the toys (bottom), push single pieces into the slot in the body sandwich.

DINOSAURS, SHIPS, AND TRAINS can be made from the parts of this simple building toy (left). The different shapes are cut from 1/8-inch lauan plywood. The finished toys stand upright when inserted into 1/8-inch wide and 1/2-inch deep slots cut into short lengths of 1 by 3 lumber.

Catapult...For Storming a Castle

A worn hacksaw blade wrapped in adhesive tape provides the launching power for this toy catapult. Complete with ammunition carrier and tow truck, the toy can be made in an evening or two by a home craftsman with a power saw.

You'll need a short length of 2 by 4 for the truck; about 3 feet of 1 by 4 to make the two bases, carrier enclosure, and catapult blocks; 2½ feet of ³⁄₁₆-inch doweling; a dozen 1⅛-inch-long screw eyes; the hacksaw blade; and a small screw and bolt. The units roll on wooden wheels—drawer pulls, spools, or short lengths of 1³⁄₈-inch dowel—drilled to accept the ³⁄₁₆-inch dowel axles.

To make the catapult mechanism, drill two holes ⁵⁄₁₆ inch apart in two triangular wood blocks and insert short ³⁄₁₆-inch dowels. Glue the triangles to the base. Bolt a U-shaped piece of wood to one end of the tape-covered hacksaw blade, using the blade's hole. Then slide the blade between the dowels and wood-screw the other end to the base (see drawing).

To provide easy in-line towing, cut a notch with a saw or chisel in the back of the truck and ammunition carrier to hold a standard cabinet magnet latch; affix the metal strike plates to the front of the carrier and catapult. Before gluing the second wheel on each axle, slide the axles through screw eyes positioned below each base. A nontoxic finish is optional.

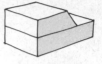

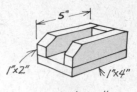

Two short lengths of 2"x4" glued

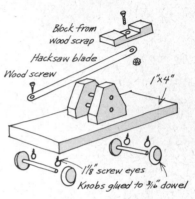

Block from wood scrap
Hacksaw blade
Wood screw
1"x4"
1⅛" screw eyes
Knobs glued to ³⁄₁₆" dowel

YOUNG MEDIEVALISTS might like to add this catapult (left) to their collections of knights and castles. The catapult gets its launching power from a hacksaw blade wrapped with tape. You make it from pieces of scrap wood (above). Be sure to use soft wood for the ammunition and sand off all sharp edges and corners. Leave natural or finish with nontoxic paint.

Building Blocks

Almost all children enjoy building blocks. You can easily make a set of blocks just by cutting 1 by 2 or other lumber into different shapes and lengths which can be stacked on top of one another. In this set, the blocks are drilled with holes so they can be connected with lengths of dowel.

The blocks are 4 and 6-inch lengths of 1 by 2-inch pine. (Any wood can be used: hardwood is best because it won't splinter easily, but a softwood such as fir is less expensive.) Drill a number of ½-inch holes in the sides and edges of each block to accept ³⁄₈-inch dowels. Space the holes consistently so the blocks can be connected in a variety of ways. Sand the surfaces and edges. Finish the blocks if you wish. The dowels can be of any length. In this set they are 8, 6, 4, and 2 inches.

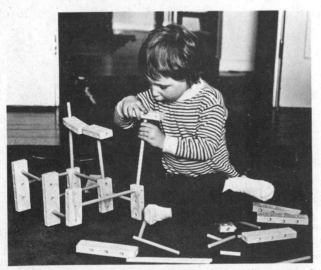

DRILLING HOLES IN BLOCKS of wood so they can be connected with dowels makes entertaining building blocks.

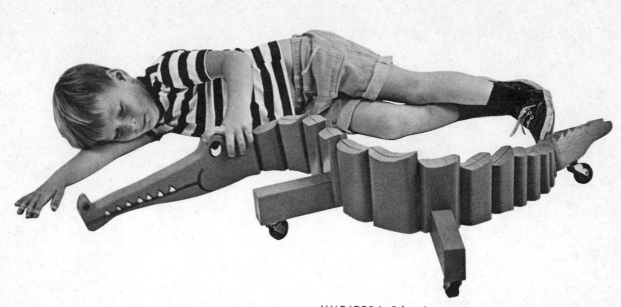

ALLIGATOR is 5 feet long and was cut into sixteen sections. A small caster was attached to his tail for support.

Wiggling Beasts on Wheels

Children will especially enjoy pulling these toys around because they wiggle and curl as they go. You build in the wiggle by making two identical body shapes, cutting both bodies into vertical sections, then sandwiching canvas between the bodies. The same technique can be used to create animals of almost any shape and size. For each of the animals shown here, you'll need two pieces of 1 by 12-inch lumber for the body and two 12-inch-long 2 by 2s for the legs (crosspieces holding the wheels).

First, draw the outline of an animal body on one of the 1 by 12s, keeping the shape simple. Draw vertical lines down the outline to divide the animal into two sections wherever his body might logically bend. Where the two crosspieces will be attached, leave the sections at least 3 inches wide.

Next, place an equal length of 1 by 12 against the 1 by 12 having the animal's body outline and temporarily fasten the two boards together by driving two nails (just deep enough to hold) through each of the marked sections. Following the vertical lines, saw the two boards into sections. Then, with the boards still nailed together, cut along the body outline of each section with a coping saw or band saw. Cut notches in the bottoms of the sections to which you will attach the crosspieces. Remove the nails holding together the two parts of each section. With a saw or power sander, remove at least a 45° wedge from the edges of adjacent sections (see drawing).

Cut a silhouette of the animal's body out of lightweight canvas, making it about 1/4 inch smaller all around than the outline of the animal. Lay one complete set of wood body sections on a table with the insides facing up. Leave a ½-inch space between each section. Centering the canvas on top, carefully position the other set of wooden sections on top of the canvas. Being careful of alignment, drive several 4-penny finishing nails into each section.

To make the legs, drill holes in each end of the two 2 by 2s and attach a caster housing in each hole. Secure the legs to the body sections with 3-inch wood screws.

To finish the animal, sink the nails and fill them over with wood putty. Sand all surfaces of the wood, then paint the animal with nontoxic paint. Add ears and a tail if you wish. Screw a small eyehook into the animal's nose for a pull cord and snap the casters into their housings in the legs.

DOCILE ELEPHANT (right) was cut into five sections. Two 2 by 2s with casters on the ends were mounted on the second and last sections. The ears can be cut from felt or leather; glue and tack them to the top of his head.

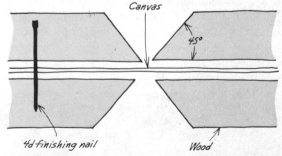

HEAD AND NECK of this ornery looking camel are not cut into sections as is the rest of the body. A fifth caster, mounted just in front of the first section, supports the head and neck.

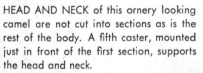

COUNTER-SUNK finishing nails hold canvas tightly between the wooden sections. Angled edges of the sections allow animals to make tight turns.

Cork Toy for the Bathtub

This easy-to-make toy is neither fish nor fowl and not quite sea serpent, but it does float, and it's fine for a bathtub toy. The toy is made from corks: five fishing floats and small cork balls that are available at import stores and ship's chandlery shops. Just string the corks onto an elastic cord, knotting it at each end. The button eyes are sewn onto the ends of the cork. For interesting variety, you might try carving the corks with a knife or using corks of different shapes and sizes. You can paint the corks in bright colors with waterproof nontoxic paint or leave them natural.

NEITHER FISH NOR FOWL, bathtub toy was made by stringing fishing floats onto cord. Knot ends of cord, add button eyes.

Fat Little Lambs with Popcorn Wool

Fat wooden lambs are made from a combination of familiar materials: popcorn and dowels. To create a flock of nine lambs, you'll need an assortment of 36-inch-long dowels in $1^1/_4$, 1, $^3/_8$, and $^1/_4$-inch diameters, white glue, white nontoxic paint, and a bowl of popcorn.

   Saw the $1^1/_4$-inch dowel into nine bodies, each $2^1/_4$ inches long. Make a diagonal cut on one end of each length so the head can be glued on firmly. Use the $^3/_8$-inch-diameter dowel to make 36 legs, each $^7/_8$ inch long; cut one end of each leg diagonally. Cut 1-inch-long heads from the 1-inch dowel. Using a chisel, split off $^1/_4$ inch to make a flat side for gluing. The ears are 18 pieces of $^1/_4$-inch dowel cut $^3/_8$ inch long. Make a diagonal cut on one end of each leg. Before assembling, sand all the dowels.

   Glue the legs to the body, then add the head and ears. Paint the lambs. Dip the popcorn in white glue, then fit the kernels tightly onto the back of each lamb. If your child likes to chew on toys, you might prefer to leave off the popcorn.

YOU CAN ASSEMBLE a flock of lambs (below left) with dowels of various diameters and lengths (below). Paint the lambs white, then glue popcorn onto their backs for wool. If your child chews toys, you might want to leave off the popcorn or use the lambs only for room decorations.

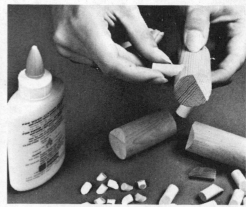

Jigsaw Puzzle

No special tools are necessary to make a puzzle like this one—only a jigsaw. This puzzle is a map of the child's neighborhood, but it could just as easily be a colorful print or even a piece of the child's own artwork.

If you decide upon a map, use a simple, easy-to-read map of your city. After labeling the places important to your child (his school, friend's house, parks) on the map, have a photostatic enlargement made of the area containing your neighborhood (look under "Photo Copying" in the yellow pages of the phone book). If you choose a print or picture, it probably won't need enlarging.

Use either water-thinned white glue or photo mounting tissue (available at camera shops) to attach the map to ½-inch-thick plywood or hardboard.

If contrast is needed in the puzzle, draw a continuous line around the edges with a colored felt marking pen. Mark main streets on the map with other colors.

With the jigsaw, cut the puzzle into large simple pieces that will be easy for a young child to put together. This puzzle is 11 by 14 inches and was cut into 25 odd-shaped pieces.

JIGSAW PUZZLES can be made easily by gluing a print or drawing onto plywood or hardboard, then cutting it into large sections with a jigsaw or coping saw. This puzzle was made with a map of the child's neighborhood.

A Colorful Counting Toy

A child's sense of the meaning of numbers can benefit from a simple counting device like this one—a plaything, teaching toy, and decoration. In this triangular version, the rows have 2, 4, 6, 8, 10, 12, 14, 16, and 18 disks, painted before assembly in yellow, orange, red, blue, and black.

To make a similar toy, first get the counters. You can use empty sewing spools, large wooden beads, or billiard score counters (available at sports shops). Widen the holes in the counters to just over ³⁄₁₆ inch with a power drill so they will slide onto ³⁄₁₆-inch wood doweling.

Size the frame to suit the counters, allowing 1 to 1½-inch sliding space on each row. Drill shallow ³⁄₁₆-inch holes in the sides to accept the dowels. The frame pictured here is 14 inches wide, 25 inches high; the rows are 2 inches apart. Construction required about 70 inches of doweling.

Assemble everything but the long side of the frame, then slide on the counters. Fit the long frame piece over the ends of the dowels and glue the corners.

COLORFUL TRIANGLE counting toy can hang from the ceiling or be affixed to a wall.

Mailing Tube Train

You can transform a mailing tube into a toy train. Its spool wheels actually turn, and it is probably as much fun to make as it is to play with.

If you plan to ship the train, it can be mailed in a 3-inch mailing tube, if you use a 2½-inch tube for the train. Besides the 2½-inch mailing tube for the car bodies, you'll need thread spools for the wheels, ¼-inch dowel for axles, a 1¼-inch tube, toothpicks, paper clips, and brass paper fasteners.

The cars are easiest to cut out if you use a band or jigsaw or a small sharp knife. Use a sharp knife to cut out the windows. The cut-out from the tender makes the top of the engine cab. Cut the stack, steam dome, and tank car top from the small 1¼-inch tube. Cardboard disks, glued onto the ends of the tube sections, form the front and back of each car. Place the disks ½ inch inside the tubes to leave space for the couplings—two small paper clips secured to the cars with brass paper fasteners. The dowel axles go through holes cut in the tube. The wheels are glued onto the ends of the dowels.

Before painting the train, assemble the parts. Use only a tiny dot of glue to hold those parts of the train that will be dismantled for shipping in the mailing tube.

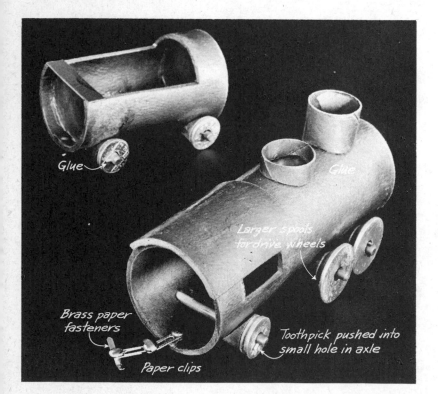

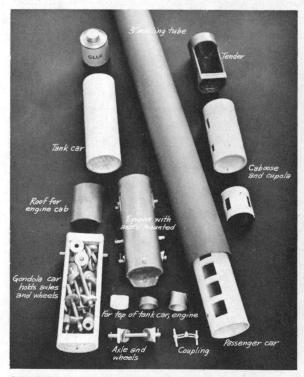

CYLINDRICAL MAILING TUBES were converted into this toy train (top). For a Christmas or birthday surprise, the partially assembled train can be mailed in a tube slightly larger than that used for the train's body (bottom). Close-up photograph of engine and tender (left) shows construction.

Portable Drawing Table

The top of this toy box opens wide to become a drawing table, then slides back when the artist is finished. The box can go along in the car or be taken out onto the patio.

To make a similar toy box, cut two 11 by 17-inch sides of ½-inch plywood and two 11¼ by 12½-inch ends of 1 by 12 lumber to receive the sides. Rabbet both sides and ends to receive the bottom, which you should cut to fit from ¼-inch plywood or hardboard.

Make sliding grooves for the tops by gluing and nailing three ¼-inch-square moldings, each 11¼ inches long, to either end, or by cutting grooves with a router or a table or radial-arm saw.

Assemble the box using nails and glue. If you like, add a thin divider inside the box to separate crayons from pads of paper and coloring books (sizes up to 9 by 12 inches can be accommodated). Drill finger holes or add wooden handles to the sides of the box.

The tops are two 11¼ by about 17-inch pieces of ¼-inch hardboard. Smooth off the edges and corners with sandpaper. When the tops are together or closed, they can be secured by two pins or blunt nails. Drill six holes in each top piece—one in each corner, and one in the middle of each end. Then line these up with holes in the middle of each molding strip.

Open or closed, the pins keep the tops from sliding out of position. Holes on the corners are used when the table tops are extended. Middle holes are used when the tops are closed. Small red dots help line up the holes so the pins will drop through quickly. Take precautions if very young children will be using the box. Keep the pins tethered on strings. Colorfully painting the exterior and interior with nontoxic paint is the finishing touch. Leave the hardboard tops natural.

OUT ON THE PATIO (below) or in the car (below left), this combination toy box and drawing table will be handy for a young artist. Crayons, pencils, paper, coloring books, and other toys store inside the box.

SEE FACING PAGE FOR INSTRUCTIONS

Doll Houses

Four Story Doll House

Sized to suit the popular 11½-inch "fashion" dolls, this doll house has an elevator, four stories, and can be built in two or three evenings. The living room has a ⅛-inch-thick clear plastic window that makes a dramatic backlight. Besides the plastic, you'll need a 4 by 4-foot sheet of ½-inch plywood and another of ⅛-inch hardboard; two 4 and two 6-foot lengths of 1 by 6-inch lumber; 8 feet of 1 by 4 lumber; 20 feet of 1 by 2 lumber; nails, brads, white glue, and two magnetic cabinet latches.

Make ³⁄₁₆-inch-wide grooves, ¼ inch deep, in the elevator-facing edges of the 1 by 6 walls to let the elevator slide freely. Saw ⅛-inch-wide grooves in the other 1 by 6s and the 1 by 1s to hold the hardboard and plastic panels. For a neat, strong job, rabbet the 1 by 6s for each floor and for the hardboard back. Use 1 by 2 lumber or ½-inch-thick base molding to edge the roof (four sides), deck (two sides), and each floor (front only).

FROM SUN DECK TO GARAGE, this town house for dolls (above, facing page) provides four levels for play. Construction is shown in the drawings below. Cut grooves in 1 by 6s with a power saw.

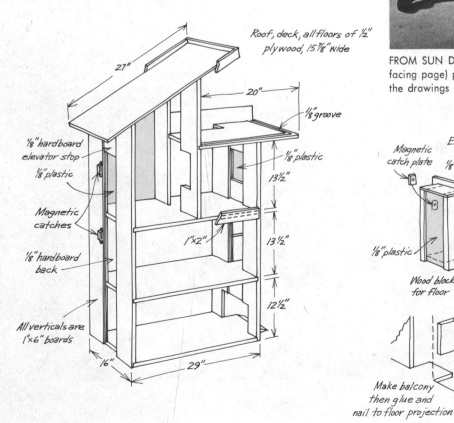

Roof, deck, all floors of ½" plywood, 15⅞" wide

27"

20"

⅛" groove

⅛" plastic

13½"

⅛" hardboard elevator stop

⅛" plastic

Magnetic catches

1"x2"

13½"

⅛" hardboard back

12½"

All verticals are 1"x6" boards

16"

29"

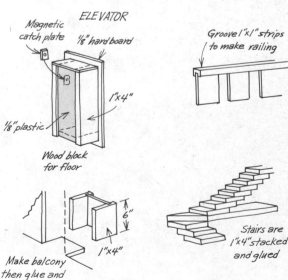

ELEVATOR

Magnetic catch plate

⅛" hardboard

1"x4"

⅛" plastic

Wood block for floor

Groove 1"x1" strips to make railing

Make balcony then glue and nail to floor projection

6"

1"x4"

Stairs are 1"x4" stacked and glued

Bookshelf Doll House

This doll house is designed like a bookshelf. You hang it on a wall where its two shelves—floors—will be at a comfortable height for its young owner. The two-story plan includes the luxury of an elevator. A cantilevered balcony overlooks the patio. Oversize doors and open hallways along the front side greatly increase freedom of movement within the house.

The scale of the doll house is $3/4$ inch to 1 foot. As detailed in the diagram, construction is quite simple. Most of the house is made of $1/4$-inch plywood. Philippine mahogany plywood is best, and you'll use about two-thirds of a 4 by 8-foot sheet.

Cut the plywood floors, partitions, and ends 10 inches wide with the grain running lengthwise on the floors and vertically on the walls. Cut out all doorways and windows before assembly and cut a $3 1/4$ by $3 1/4$-inch opening in the upper floor for the elevator. Draw lines on the two floors where the partitions will go and assemble the doll house with $3/4$-inch number 20 wire nails and white glue.

Attach the lower partitions to the lower floor, nailing from below, then attach the two-story left side. Attach the upper-story partitions to the upper floor (again nailing from below). Note from the drawings that the second-story partitions alongside the elevator shaft are jogged $1/4$ inch from those below. Last, glue and nail (from above) the upper floor to the left side and to the lower-floor partitions.

Lay the partially-assembled house on its back side on a piece of plywood and mark off the back wall.

Cut out the wall, then glue and nail it in place. Next, build the elevator and slip it into its shaft. Its four front trim pieces and two second-story guide pieces are simply glued in place.

This doll house has a bubble skylight (optional) in the bathroom roof. It is the clear plastic lid from a small box of straight pins. Simply cut out a hole in the roof and glue the lid in place.

Glue and nail the six roof beams to the tops of the three bearing walls. Then attach the two roof sections, after placing glue on the top edges of all four walls. Let the roof overlap the edge of the rear wall. With the elevator at the first floor level, center and drill a small hole through its floor and the first floor at the same time for alignment. Enlarge the hole through the first floor to $3/8$ inch. Slide the elevator's dowel through that hole and attach it to the elevator with glue and a screw driven through the small hole in its floor.

Glue the fireplace and chimney top in place. Finish the roof by painting it with white glue, thinned slightly with water, and sprinkling it with nutty-grain dry breakfast cereal. Paint over this "rock" roof with white glue and allow it to harden.

Add balcony railings and $1/4$ by $3/4$-inch strips of plywood or mahogany to the front edges of the floors and to the end of the patio. After you glue a 3 by 6-inch piece of plywood to the underside of the first floor so it projects to form an entry step, the doll house is ready for furniture.

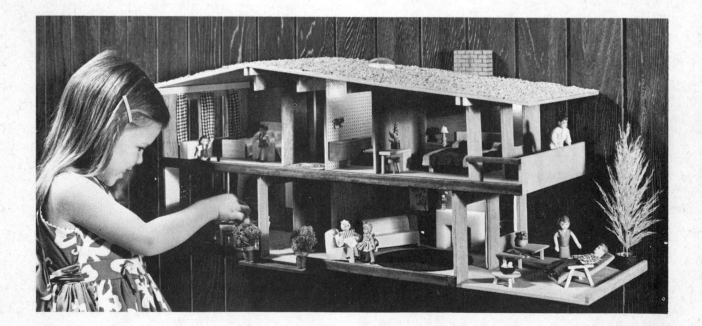

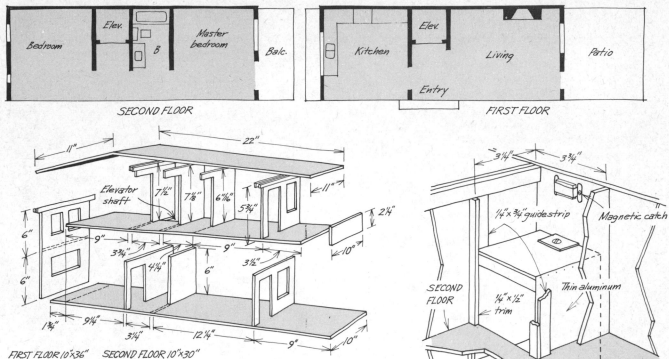

SECOND FLOOR — Bedroom · Elev. · B · Master bedroom · Balc.

FIRST FLOOR — Kitchen · Elev. · Living · Patio · Entry

Elevator shaft

7½" · 7⅞" · 6¹¹⁄₁₆" · 5¾" · 11"

2¼"

6" · 9" · 9" · 10"

3¾" · 4¼" · 6" · 3½"

6"

1¾" · 9¼" · 10"

3¼" · 12¼" · 9"

FIRST FLOOR 10"×36"   SECOND FLOOR 10"×30"

3¼" · 3¾"

¼" × ¾" guidestrip

Magnetic catch

SECOND FLOOR

¼" × ½" trim

Thin aluminum

FIRST FLOOR

¼" × ¼" trim

⅜" hardwood dowel

ELEVATOR   Half of wood spool

FLOOR PLAN AND CONSTRUCTION. Top drawing: floor plans. Drawing immediately above: framing details (back wall and floor trim omitted for clarity); cut doors 3" by 5". Right: elevator is made of ¼" plywood; use aluminum sheeting or plywood for sides. Elevator should fit fairly loosely. Adjust magnetic catch on wall so elevator floor is level with 2nd floor when in up position.

INTERIOR DETAILS of doll house are shown in the photographs below. Left photo (left side of house): use adhesive backed contact paper for kitchen floor. Center photo (center of house): elevator pushes up with a dowel. Right photo (right side of house): fireplace is cut from styrene foam.

The Hillside Doll House

Like many real homes, this doll house is built on a hillside—in this case, a plywood hill. Two sections of the roof, two wall sections on the rear, and a lower "drawer" floor on the front open to give access to small hands throughout the house. The plywood hillside provides space beneath the house for a large storage drawer that opens from the back of the house.

The doll house was made mainly of 1/4-inch mahogany plywood. Lines drawn on the fine-grained plywood with a soft pencil simulate a shingle exterior. The "shingles" were varnished by spray can.

In building the house, follow the diagram and photographs. Leave the doors and windows of the house open. Use small ornamental brass hinges on the roof and the hinging walls with magnetic catches to hold them closed. Coarse, open-grit sandpaper glued onto plywood forms the "rock" roof. Glue artificial grass over the hillside slope.

At the house's "drawer" level, install a plywood floor as elsewhere, then build a simple drawer, sized according to the space available, to slide over it. To provide a skylight over the living room's large window, glue a piece of white plastic in place. Make the stairways out of slanting pieces of plywood, drawing in the steps with pencil. Build a ramp in the back of the house leading to the carport.

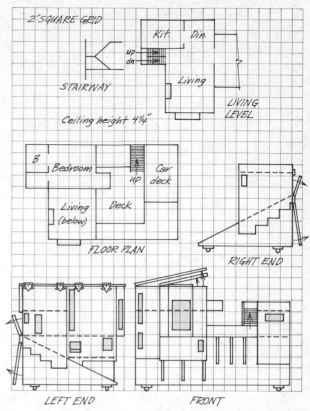

ENLARGE GRID SQUARES to 2 inches square for a doll house scale of 1/2 inch to 1 foot. You can make them larger or smaller, if you wish, to suit doll size.

PROUD HOME OWNER rearranges the furnishings on her elevated deck —between the studio at right and her three-story house at left. Back walls and roof are hinged to provide access inside.

FOR PLAY INSIDE, roof is hinged in two sections. It swings down on her side, giving access to bedroom and living areas. Housekeeping drawer is beneath the house.

A Doll's House-trailer

Rolling along to a new "campsite" down the street is fun for the owners of this doll house-trailer. Essentially, it is a simple plywood box that slips over the old red wagon. This one is designed for a 17 by 36-inch wagon bed.

To make a doll house-trailer, rip a 4 by 8-foot sheet of ¹/₂-inch plywood into two 18-inch by 8-foot pieces. From one 18-inch piece, cut two 37-inch-long sides; from the other, cut the 18-inch-square front and back and the 36-inch floor. From the leftover plywood, cut two 8 by 18-inch beds; the 8-inch-square seat back; the 8-inch-square table top; and the closet pieces, which are two 3¹/₂ by 13-inch sides, a 6 by 13-inch back, and a 3¹/₂ by 6-inch top. From the 12-inch by 8-foot piece of remaining plywood, cut four 5 by 20-inch pieces to make the counter; two 7 by 12-inch doors; and the 1 by 4¹/₄-inch table leg. Cut the one 4¹/₂-inch and three 8-inch seats from a 4 by 4. Cut the 18-inch-long dashboard from 2 by 2 stock. Bevel one face of the dashboard.

The windows are 7 inches square. Drill a 1¹/₄-inch hole for each corner of the windows and cut them out with a keyhole saw. In one of the side pieces, cut an opening to match the two 7 by 12-inch doors, 8¹/₂ inches in from the back edge and 1 inch down from the top. Cut out the wheel wells.

When assembling the body, lap the sides over the ends and position the floor 5 inches up from the bottom edge to hide the wagon bed. Glue and nail the parts together.

Assemble the table in the trailer by hinging a leg to the table top and hinging the table top to the wall. Glue the dashboard to the front at the height of the seat. Attach drawer pulls to the doors for handles and hang the doors with pin hinges. Glue the four counter pieces together, leaving the ends open for storage. Glue the closet pieces together, then add a plywood shelf and a ¹/₄-inch dowel clothes bar. Sand the edges and corners and finish with a sealer or nontoxic paint.

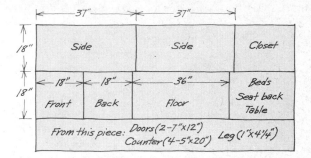

ONE SHEET of plywood can be cut (as shown above) into doll house parts. Finished doll house slips over bed of a wagon. Below: doll house interior. Black tape marks counters; magnetic catch holds doors closed.

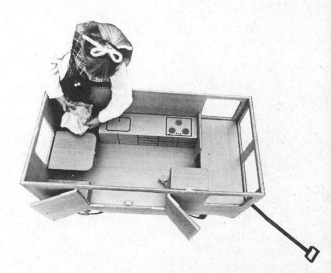

This Doll House Revolves

Two or more children could play with this doll house without getting in each other's way. Each room is on a stage—open and wide—and the entire house revolves smoothly on ball bearings. Small hands can pass things through the oversize doors. There is also an inside patio. The scale is ³/₄-inch to 1 foot.

To lay out the floor, drive two brads 18 inches apart through a yardstick to make a compass. Draw and cut the 36-inch circle on a piece of plywood, then draw arcs on its circumference to divide it into six equal parts—one for each room. Draw in room lines.

Assemble the house with white glue and small wire nails (see drawing). The rear walls are beveled on the sides to butt flat against the side walls. This house is painted in a single color. While the paint is still wet, the roof is sprinkled with coarse sand to simulate gravel. Furnish the rooms with commercial doll house furniture sold in toy stores or make furniture yourself out of a soft wood such as balsa.

Here are some construction hints for a few of the rooms. *Kitchen:* The kitchen has three doorways, and, as in all of the rooms, the opening has a 1¹/₄-inch plywood strip running across the bottom of the outer edge. *Living room:* The fireplace hood is a small plastic funnel and a 1-inch-diameter metal tube, glued together and to the roof. The firepit is a telescoping drinking cup. All of the pieces are painted black. *Bath and laundry rooms:* The bath and laundry are separated by a partition. The cabinets along the wall of the laundry room are blocks of soft wood outlined with pencil. *Patio, entry:* The entrance garden and patio floor are first painted brick red. Then a grass mat and rubber shrubs (from a hobby store) are glued in place. The trunk of the small tree in the middle of the patio is the axle bolt from the house's base, camouflaged with glued-on "branches" and green paint. Its planter is a spray can lid.

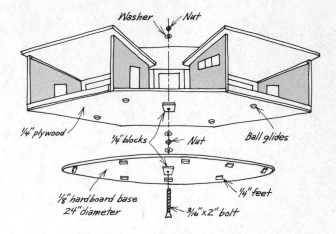

HOUSE REVOLVES on four furniture ball glides (single rolling ball bearings) set in the floor. The ball glides roll against a hardboard base to which the house is bolted.

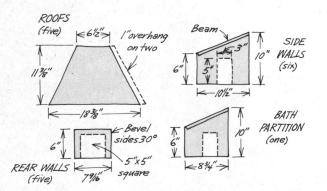

WALLS AND PARTITIONS are cut from ¼-inch plywood. After cutting them out, glue and nail to hexagonal floor.

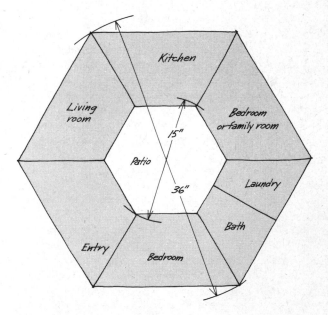

HEXAGONAL FLOOR starts as a 36-inch circle of plywood. Inner hexagon (15-inch diameter) creates the inner patio.

EXPOSED ROOMS of this doll house make play easy, especially since the whole house revolves on its base (see drawings at left). Hexagonal floor is divided into rooms by panels of plywood. Front of each room is left open. Cut doorways in each room divider.

LIVING ROOM of this house was furnished with balsa wood furniture similar to pieces described on page 25.

ENTRY AND PATIO aren't covered by a roof. Plants and grass from hobby store were added after a brick-red paint job.

KITCHEN has three doorways. As in all other rooms, the outer edge is bordered by a 1¼-inch plywood strip.

BATH AND LAUNDRY rooms are separated by an extra wall. Furnishings were purchased at a toy store.

The Reach-into Doll House

Here's a really big doll house—over 4 feet long with three levels. Several children can play with it at one time. Yet, the doll house comes apart easily to be stored away or transported as a fairly flat package. You just lift off the roof and the circular stairway, unscrew the second floor, and remove the dowels from the lower floor from underneath.

The simple construction allows you to build it to any floor plan desired and to scale it up or down in size to fit different dolls. This one is scaled 1 inch to 1 foot.

The two floors and roof are simply three pieces of ½-inch plywood, the upper two pieces being larger to provide overhangs. They are framed with ½-inch dowel "poles," spaced about 5 inches apart, with cotter pins on the lower ends to keep all the weight on the dowels. Here and there, two of the loose dowels are slotted lengthwise and joined with glued-on ⅛-inch plywood partitions to make rooms and hold up the roof.

Lauan plywood, finished with a coat of clear floor wax, was used for the decks and panels. The circular stairway slips down through large holes in the roof and second floor, resting in a ½-inch hole in the first floor. Make the railings out of hardwood or solid plywood. Attach the railings to the doll house with white glue and brads.

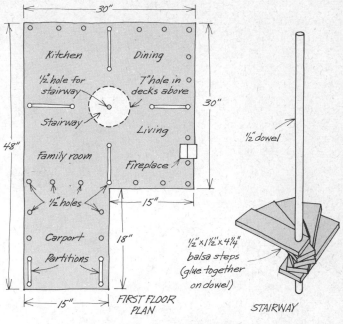

FIRST FLOOR PLAN (left) shows placement of dowels supporting second floor and partitions. Stairway (right) is balsa planks drilled and glued to a dowel.

LARGE AND ROOMY, this doll house has no obstructing walls.

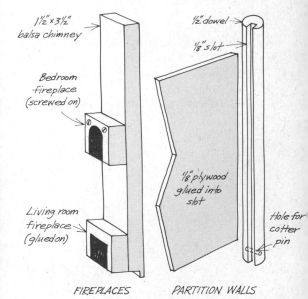

FIREPLACES AND PARTITIONS are shown in the art above. Place partitions between any of the supporting dowels you want. New rooms can be created by placing partitioned dowels differently.

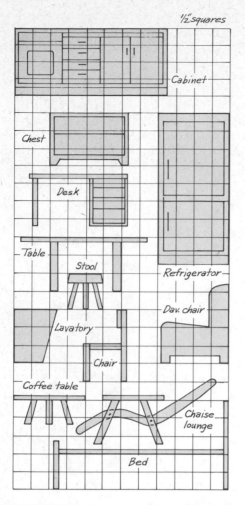

½" squares

Cabinet

Chest

Desk

Table

Stool

Refrigerator

Dav. chair

Lavatory

Chair

Coffee table

Chaise lounge

Bed

MANY POSSIBILITIES for furniture are shown above, below right. If you are furnishing an entire doll house, keep the scale of all pieces the same. Paint finished furniture with nontoxic paint or leave it natural. Pencil or paint on details.

Doll House Furnishings

When you delight a child with a doll house, the youngster will probably want to move the dolls in right away. Almost every type of doll house furnishing can be purchased at a toy store, but if you'd prefer to make them yourself, here are some ideas.

The doll house furniture shown here was made from balsa wood. This soft, light wood can easily be shaped and is strong enough to hold up if you avoid using the very thin model airplane stock.

Most hobby shops and hardware stores carry balsa wood in a variety of sizes and shapes for model making. For table tops and benches, choose fairly thick planks (about ⅛ inch) and use sturdy balsa sticks for legs. Attach the parts with white glue, holding them together with pins until the glue dries thoroughly. (Be sure to remove all the pins.)

Model-making balsa also comes in blocks about 2 by 4 by 12 inches in size. From these blocks you can cut sofas, overstuffed chairs, chaise lounges, chests, kitchen and bath cabinets, and appliances. A band saw will cut all of these. Most jigsaws and hand scroll saws will not adjust to a thickness equal to the length of a sofa; with such tools make sectional pieces and glue them together.

For drawers in a chest or cabinet, simply draw deep lines in the wood with a soft-lead pencil. Paint the furniture with nontoxic paint if you wish, then redraw the black lines in the grooves.

To finish the pieces, sand them smooth with very fine sandpaper. To give pieces of furniture an upholstered look, sand the pieces with medium or coarse sandpaper to create a fuzz on the balsa.

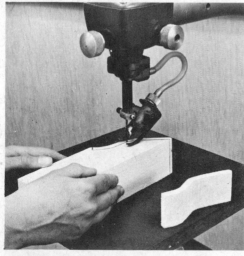

CUT OUT FURNITURE at right with a jigsaw, band-saw, or with a coping saw (above).

SEE FACING PAGE FOR INSTRUCTIONS

Things to Sew

Rag Dolls

These dolls have a soft, floppy, homemade appeal. All of them were created from the simple pattern shown in the drawing, which you can modify to suit your whim. The material for a doll can be anything from burlap to leather or fake fur and choosing the fabric is half the fun. Other materials include yarn for hair and felt for facial features and clothing. Colored felt-tipped pens might be used to add final touches on the doll's face.

To make a doll, cut out a paper pattern that roughly corresponds to the pattern shown in the drawing. It doesn't have to be exact; in fact, it doesn't even need to be symmetrical. Pin the pattern onto ½ yard of the fabric of your choice (folded in half with the right sides together), then cut it out.

Start stitching the material together at the side of the head, leaving about 7 inches open at the top of the head for stuffing the doll. Stitch the seam about ½ inch in from the edge. Clip the seams as shown in the photograph and turn the material. Fill the doll with a washable stuffing such as dacron batting.

Using an overcast stitch, sew up the opening in the doll's head. A mop of yarn hair or a felt hat will cover the stitching. Sew on yarn or felt facial features or draw them on with felt-tipped pens.

PUDGY DOLLS marching across the lawn have one thing in common: they all are made from ½ yard of material, cut according to the pattern below. Most materials can be used.

ENLARGE PATTERN SQUARES (below) to 4½ inches. Fold right sides of fabric together, pin pattern on (below center). Cut out fabric and, after stitching, clip seam allowance (below right). Turn the material right side out and stuff.

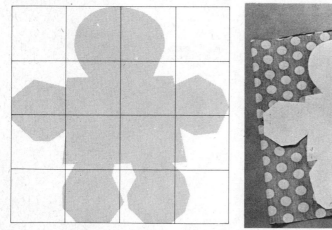

Yarn Animals

To make the fluffy animals shown here, wrap yarn around rectangular templates to create the body, 4 legs, head, and tail, and then sew the parts together. The process is shown in the photographs below.

   Start an animal by first cutting two cardboard templates to the dimensions shown in the drawing. Then wrap 4-ply yarn around the templates. Follow the numbers and lines in the drawing that indicate how many layers of yarn to wrap and the number of inches along the template to wrap. Wrap only one layer of yarn at a time, pushing the strands close together as you go. To make an animal with different colored paws, wrap ³/₄ of the leg template with the body color yarn and the rest with a contrasting color.

   After wrapping the template, sew across the center of the yarn (in the open, window-section of the template) with heavy-duty thread. Use a backstitch; make sure all of the strands are sewn. Then cut the yarn along each edge of the template. Fluff the yarn into a soft, round shape.

   After completing the seven parts, sew the ends of the head piece together and sew all of the parts onto the body. Be sure to sew through the stitching in the center of each piece rather than just through the ends of the yarn. Add facial features made from felt, yarn, or buttons.

   To make an animal with a muzzle like the lion's, wrap the yarn for the head around a cardboard template. Then, after sewing the yarn, cut the template at one end and slip off the yarn without cutting it. Sew the ends together and cut all of the loops except those in the center.

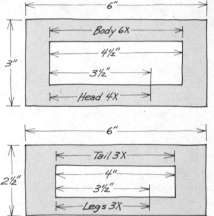

NUMBERS IN DRAWING indicate the distance and number of times to wrap the templates.

FIRST WRAP TEMPLATE (below), following lengths and thicknesses indicated in drawing. Sew through center of yarn (center), then cut the yarn where it goes over template edges (right).

Monkeys Made from Socks

For children who like to keep a menagerie of soft animals, here are monkeys made out of heavy cotton work socks. One sock forms the monkey's head, body, and legs; the other sock is cut into arms, tail, muzzle, and ears. The white heels and toes of the socks used for these monkeys create contrasting hands, feet, mouth, and tail.

Cut the socks according to the instructions in the drawings. After sewing and stuffing the parts, sew them together, adding the muzzle and ears. The little caps and jackets these monkeys are wearing can be made from brightly colored cloth scraps.

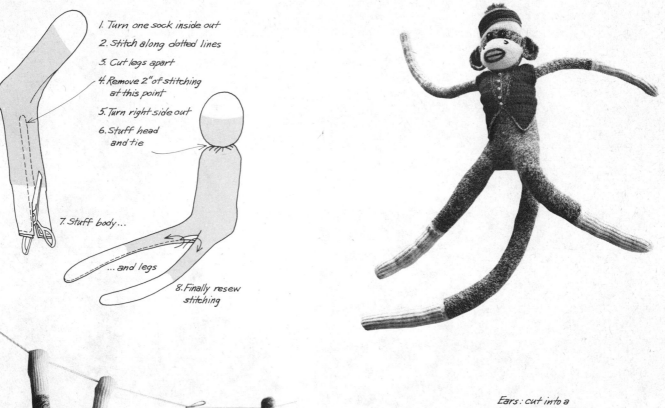

1. Turn one sock inside out
2. Stitch along dotted lines
3. Cut legs apart
4. Remove 2" of stitching at this point
5. Turn right side out
6. Stuff head and tie
7. Stuff body...
...and legs
8. Finally resew stitching

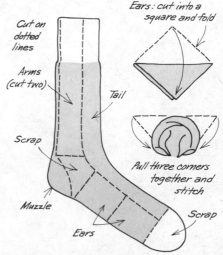

Cut on dotted lines

Arms (cut two)

Tail

Scrap

Muzzle

Ears

Scrap

Ears: cut into a square and fold

Pull three corners together and stitch

Bean Bags

Bean bags are a favorite for many tossing games. Here are some ideas and shapes you might like to use for making bean bags. The frog is made from the pattern in the drawing which can be enlarged to any size you want. The other bean bags—Mr. 5 by 5, tortoise, and clown—are different shapes you might like.

To make a bean bag, draw the shape you want onto a piece of heavy wrapping paper and cut it out for a pattern. Use this pattern to cut out two identical pieces of colorful fabric. Sew the pieces right sides together, leaving about 5 inches of the seam unsewn so the material can be turned right side out and stuffed with beans or raw rice. After filling the bean bag, sew the open section by hand. Add buttons or colorful scraps of material for facial features. The hair and the pattern on the turtle's back are yarn.

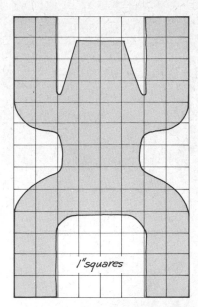

1" squares

CLASSIC PLAYTHINGS, bean bags take many forms. Those at right are two pieces of fabric cut to same whimsical shape and sewn together. Frog (below) was made from pattern above.

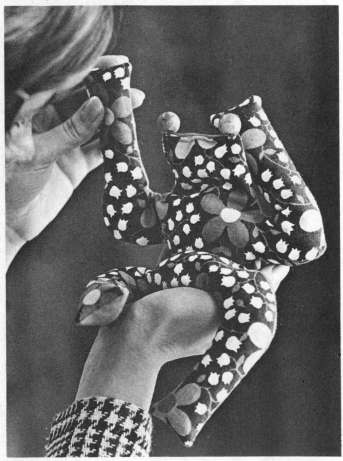

A Pair of Owls

The two owls shown here are about 12 inches tall from horn to tail and are made from the pattern in the drawing. First cut two identical body pieces from the material of your choice. Then sew the pieces together, wrong sides out, leaving a 5-inch opening along one side. Turn the material right side out and stuff with dacron batting. Use a blunt knitting needle to push the filling into corners. Sew up the side; add button eyes and a felt beak.

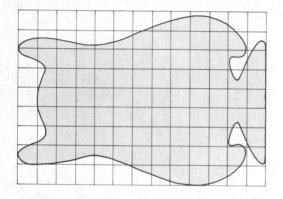

JUST OVER 1 FOOT TALL, these owls were cut according to pattern at left after squares were enlarged to 1 inch.

Patchwork Terrier

With 76 equal-sized squares of fabric, you can assemble this patchwork dog. Cut the squares any size (they are 3½ inches square on this dog); just make sure to cut them all the same size. For variety, use one printed and two coordinating solid-colored fabrics.

Assemble the squares for each side of the dog separately, following the pattern in the photograph: 6 squares for the head, 10 for the body, 2 for each leg, and 1 for the tail. Thirty squares sewn together into a single strip with ¼-inch seams connect the two sides of the dog. For each ear, sew two squares together on three sides; turn right side out and press.

With the right sides together, sew the strip around one side of the toy and then the other, inserting the ears in the proper places and leaving a 7-inch opening along one side.

Clip all the corners; turn the dog right side out, fill with dacron batting or other stuffing, then sew up the opening with a blind stitch. Tack the left top corner of each ear down to the head about ½ inch in from the seam to form a triangle. For the eyes, cut two pieces of felt in a daisy pattern and glue them onto the appropriate spot on each side of the head. Then sew a button in the middle of each.

PATTERNED AND CONTRASTING MATERIALS were used for this patchwork dog. Squares were staggered so no two of the same material were together. Reverse the pattern for the other side.

One Chicken After Another

For young children who love to take things apart and put them back together again, this felt nesting toy is a delight. The child begins by unzipping the back of a rooster, then goes on to open three progressively smaller chicks. Each is unfastened differently, and there's an egg inside the smallest chick.

The body size of each chick depends on the size of the next largest chick. Start with the largest bird, drawing its oval body, any size you like, onto tracing paper. About ½ inch inside the oval, draw a second body oval for the next chick. Make each of the successively smaller chicks the same way, except the one with snaps described below. Use brightly colored pieces of felt for all parts, including wings, eyes, and a crack in the egg. Cut two matching pieces for each body.

Each chick has a different opening. The rooster has a zipper opening. Select a zipper to fit the body you've cut, then stitch it to the back section. To make the button chick, cut a flap in the back, then add a rectangular insert of felt to the bottom of the top half and stitch it on. Sew on the buttons and make buttonholes in the flap. The next smaller chick has snaps. When making a pattern for the snap chick, allow for a flap on the back by drawing a line through the middle and adding ½ inch to the top and bottom halves. Sew on the snaps. The smallest chick is laced. Cut three or four slits in the felt for lace or a shoestring.

NESTING CHICKENS, one inside another, teach children how to zip, snap, button, lace, and to distinguish different-sized objects.

A ROOSTER, THREE CHICKS, AND AN EGG (top) — each diminishing in size — fit one inside the next. Bottom: the rooster zips, the next chick buttons, the middle chick snaps, the last one laces. An egg with an appliqued crack fits inside the smallest chick. Each part is basically just two pieces of felt sewn together.

Jump Rope Handles

Giving the old-fashioned jump rope a pair of whimsical handles will appeal to youngsters who spend a lot of time jumping to favorite verses. You also might offer one to basketball players and jogging enthusiasts.

Except for the work gloves, the handles shown here were cut from colorful felt. Trace the shape of the handle you want onto a piece of paper and, using this pattern, cut out two identical pieces of felt. Add ears, noses, spots, and other details cut from felt to complete the design. Whipstitch the two parts together, right sides out, leaving an opening for the rope. Insert the end of the rope into the handle, stuff around it with polyester fiber or cotton, then complete the stitching, going through the rope several times where it goes into the handle. The work gloves are just stuffed with cotton and secured at the wrist with a tight knot. For the jump rope, use white cotton clothesline or nylon rope, available in brilliant colors.

IMAGINATIVE BEASTS and carrot are each just two pieces of felt sewn together and stuffed, with the rope inserted and sewn in one end. The hand is a stuffed work glove with the rope tied onto the end.

Christmas Stockings

Christmas stockings (or shoes, boots, skates—even a bare foot) will appeal to a child's whimsy at Christmastime. The stockings shown here are made of felt and require very little time and effort to complete. All you do is decide on a design, cut out the felt, and sew.

First draw the basic shape of the stocking idea you want onto two pieces of felt. Ideas for stockings can be taken from any kind of footwear: the child's favorite hobby, hero, or sport might suggest ideas. In designing the stocking, be sure to make it wide enough to accommodate Santa's hand. The stockings shown here measure 11½ inches from heel to toe and 14 inches from heel to top. Cut out the felt pieces and applique other pieces of colorful materials onto them to complete the design. Sew the two parts together.

FROM FLOWERED SOCK to cowboy boot, the stockings shown here were cut from felt and decorated with appliqued felt and pompons.

Child's Art on a Pillow

SNAIL, SUN, and a smiling row of posies, each taken from a child's drawing, decorate these burlap throw pillows.

Looking for a way to preserve your child's art? Enlarging the art and appliqueing it onto pillows is one answer. The pillows shown here are burlap appliqued onto burlap backing. Sailcloth, denim, or felt could also be used. Details of the designs are yarn, buttons, and patches of cloth.

Instead of interpreting an entire picture, choose one or two portions. Enlarge these parts to fit the pillow backing, broadening the lines where necessary. Cut out the pieces for applique from single-color material and stitch them to the background material, using a regular machine stitch. If your machine will make a zigzag stitch, use it to bind in the raw edges of the fabric; otherwise, bind them by hand, using a buttonhole or outline stitch.

Where the design suggests loops, make them out of yarn, sewing it on with a large needle. Sew the two parts of the pillow together along three sides, right sides together. Turn the pillow right side out and stuff with dacron batting. Close the unsewn side with a slip stitch. If you've made the pillow out of burlap, line it with sheeting before sewing to prevent the stuffing from falling out.

FOR TELLING TIME, this pillow has hands that button onto the numbers — appliqued or drawn onto cloth-covered buttons.

A Pillow Clock

What child wouldn't want a double-duty pillow and clock with movable hands? Begin with 13 shank cover-your-own buttons, 1½ inches in diameter. Cover the buttons with solid-colored fabrics and draw or applique numbers on 12 of them.

Cut two 16-inch-diameter circles of fabric. On the right side of one circle, arrange and sew the 12 numbered buttons, 3 inches in from the fabric's outer edge. Sew the 13th button to the center of the fabric.

With the right sides of the two circles together (buttons inside), stitch a ½-inch-deep seam around the circumference; leave a 5-inch opening. Turn the farbic right side out, stuff, and handstitch closed.

Cut two 9 by 1¼-inch strips of fabric for the minute hand and two 7½ by 1¼-inch strips for the hour hand. Make a point at one end of each strip. Sew matching strips together (right sides out) with a zigzag stitch or hand-sewn buttonhole stitch. Make two buttonholes on each hand: one at the square ends for the center of the clock, another at the pointed ends for the numbers. Let the minute hand extend about 1 inch beyond the hour hand.

IMITATION FUR BEAR can be a spread, or if coated with latex, a rug.
Pieces are just cut out (see pattern below) and glued together.

Woolly "Bear Spread"

You don't have to be able to sew to make this friendly bear for a favorite youngster. You just cut him out of imitation fur, then glue the felt features in place. Imitation fur materials are available at large yardage goods stores and theatrical supply stores. They are generally made out of acrylic pile on cotton backing. If you can avoid it, don't buy fabric that has been backed with latex. When you attach the feet, the latex hinders the glue from penetrating the fibers and making a good bond. You can coat the finished bear with latex yourself, if you wish to make it into a rug. (Latex rug backing, or seaming cement, is available from floor covering stores. You apply it to the back of the material with a brush and let it dry; it provides a non-slip backing.)

You'll use 2 yards of 54 or 56-inch-wide imitation fur for the bear's body and ears, as well as felt scraps for his nose, eyes, paws, and the backs of his ears. You'll also need a generous supply of white glue.

Make a paper pattern, pin it to the fur, and cut out the body of the bear. Cut two ears from scraps of the fur. From felt, cut four paws, two eyes, a nose, and two more ears. Using a generous amount of white glue and applying pressure, glue the paws, eyes, and nose into position on the body.

To make the ears, glue the felt backing to the fur pieces, then cut a slit as shown in the drawing. Lap the fabric over to the dotted line in the drawing and glue in place. When dry, glue the ears to the bear, weighting them down until the glue is completely dry.

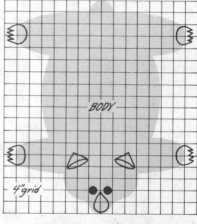

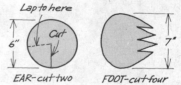

ENLARGE THE SQUARES to 4 inches; cut the body from imitation fur and the features from felt.

Slipover Smock for a Painter

As a cover-up for little girls who like painting and other messy activities, this smock slips over a dress or swimsuit before the young artist or cook begins work. Its simplicity recommends it. The duck design on the front, or your own big, bold decoration, is optional.

For a size 6 smock, you'll need ⅔ yard of 45-inch cotton lining, ⅔ yard of 45-inch sailcloth, two metal buckles, and contrasting fabric for applique. Follow the pattern to cut the shift and cotton lining. Before stitching them together, applique the duck or your own design onto the front of the smock. If you spray the fabric shapes with liquid starch and iron them, they will be stiff and won't curl or ravel. Machine-baste the design in place with a medium width and medium length zigzag stitch. Use a satin stitch over this basting line for a durable, finished edge.

To sew the smock: stitch the back neckline dart (taper from ¼ inch at the widest point). The smock is self-lined; you stitch the right sides together, back and back lining, front and front lining. Leave an opening for turning at the center of the lower edges and at the shoulder edges, stitching only to within ⅝ inch of the neck and shoulder edges. Turn the material.

Finish the neck by stitching front and back at the shoulder seams. Be careful not to catch the lining. Slip-stitch shoulder edges of lining together; slip-stitch opening at lower edge. Edge-stitch the whole smock ⅛ inch from all finished edges. Sew buckles to back extensions. Use eyelets if you wish, but the front extensions can just slip through the buckles; they stay in place and resist some stress.

PULL-OVER SMOCK might be just what your young artist needs. This one was cut from 45-inch fabric according to the pattern (right). Applique duck or your own design to front.

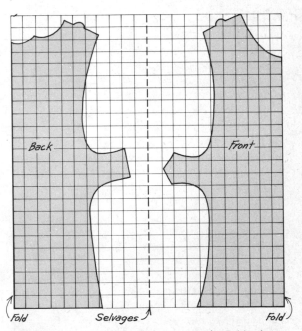

FOR SIZE 6 enlarge the squares to 1 inch. Fold selvage edges of 45-inch fabric to center and cut. For larger sizes, widen at folds, then lengthen hem.

A BUDDING YOUNG COOK should wear this gay, colorful apron with pride. Flower pot, appliqued in place, doubles as pocket.

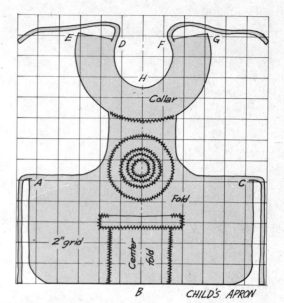

GRAY AREAS indicate apron body, applique, bias tape. Zigzag lines are machine zigzag stitch.

An Apron for a Young Cook

The three-year-old in this photograph wouldn't dream of taking on a cooking or coloring project without her bright-colored apron. To make a similar apron for a youngster you know, you'll need ²/₃ yard of sturdy fabric for the apron, a 10 by 20-inch piece of fabric for the collar and flower (the biggest flower circle is 6 inches in diameter), and about 4¹/₂ yards of bias tape.

First enlarge the pattern so that it will fit your child. (If you wish, make a muslin apron to check the fit.) Cut the apron fabric along the outline of the entire apron as shown in the pattern. Cut applique fabrics with an additional ¹/₂-inch margin around each outline to be appliqued. Cut out the collar and cut two to four flower circles of diminishing sizes. Cut the flower pot 1 inch longer than shown in the pattern.

Fold the pot rim down 1 inch over the top of the pot into the position shown in the pattern. Press the rim and stitch to pot (see drawing). Applique pot to apron, leaving a 5¹/₂-inch opening at the top for the pocket. Applique flower circles to the apron. Fashion the flower stem by making a zigzag stitch from the bottom of the flower to 1 inch underneath the pot rim. Attach the bottom of the collar to the apron.

To bind the raw edges of the apron, sew 1¹/₄ yards of bias tape from A to B to C. Cut two 1-yard lengths of tape and sew one length from D to E to A; sew the other length from F to G to C. Leave two strips, each about 10 inches long, at points A and C for waist ties and continue stitching the edges of the tape together to finish the ties. Stitch 1 yard of tape from D to H to F; leave two strips, each about 10 inches long, at D and F, then stitch the edges of the tape together to finish the ties.

SEE FACING PAGE FOR INSTRUCTIONS

Performing Toys

Marionettes

Your young puppeteer might enjoy these marionettes. Beneath their cloth coverings, they have a skeleton of spools (125-yard size) and a 2-inch styrofoam ball for a head.

First, tie two spools together with string, about 1 inch apart, for the trunk of the body (see drawing). Thread another string, 11 inches long, through each trunk spool and tie a spool to each of the ends. Cut out two pieces of cloth for the marionette's body covering (see pattern) and sew them right sides together with a ¼-inch seam allowance. Do not sew the bottoms of the feet and arms; leave a 2-inch opening at the neck.

Turn the cloth and insert the spools through the neck, putting one in each arm and leg. Cut four 1½-inch squares of fabric. Place a square over the leg and arm openings, fold the edges under, and handsew to the end pieces.

To cover the head, cut a 6-inch square of material; put the styrofoam ball in the center, then gather and tie the corners together tightly with string. Distribute the folds in the cloth evenly to blend with facial features. (To form noses, glue cotton around the styrofoam ball before wrapping.) Insert the tied section of the head into the neck opening and sew the head and body together. For faces, sew on buttons, yarn, and felt.

To operate the marionettes, attach 18-inch lengths of strong thread to the head and body. Tie the other ends to 7-inch lengths of ¼-inch dowel.

MARIONETTES can do many things. By manipulating the strings, children make them walk, jump, bend, and even ride each other. They might be easiest for small children to work if you attach only two or three strings to each marionette.

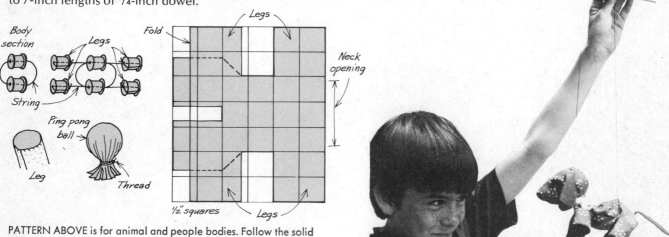

PATTERN ABOVE is for animal and people bodies. Follow the solid lines for animal bodies, dotted lines (arms point downwards) for people. Skeletons are spools tied together.

Puppets with Big Jaws

Frogs and alligators are not ordinarily welcome house guests, but even a squeamish mother wouldn't object to them as children's puppets. Made of wood and cloth, they're neither expensive nor complicated. The dimensions in the drawings are only guidelines. As long as the body fits snugly across the puppet's head and the puppet feels comfortable on your hand, you can alter the measurements to fit your materials.

For the frog with bulging eyes, you'll need two pieces of $\frac{1}{2}$-inch plywood or other wood, cut 4 inches wide and 8 inches long, two $1\frac{1}{2}$-inch-diameter round wooden drawer pulls, two hinges, paint, and $\frac{1}{2}$ yard of corduroy. Begin making the frog's head by rounding off one end of both pieces of plywood with a saw until U-shaped. Smooth the edges of the jaws with sandpaper. At the other ends, hinge the throat. Finish with nontoxic paint and let dry.

Make the frog's eyes from the two drawer pulls. For the center of the eyes, use a $\frac{3}{4}$-inch drill bit to drill a $\frac{1}{2}$-inch-deep hole in each. Sand and paint the insides of both holes with dark paint. (Or, if you prefer, just paint the center of each eye.) Glue the eyeballs to the upper jaw 5 inches from the hinges.

To make the cloth body, cut one piece of corduroy the size of the frog body pattern. This is the top cloth. Cut the bottom cloth to match the smaller, dotted pattern. You can make an attractive lining for the body by cutting a piece of cotton print as shown in the drawing. Turn the straight edges of both corduroy pieces under about $\frac{1}{2}$ inch where the cloth will be attached to the wood, then stitch to make a hem.

Pin the top and bottom pieces of corduroy, right sides together. If you made a lining, put it right side down on top of the bottom piece and sew around the edge of the circle. If not, stitch the sides of the overlapping circular section and hem the remaining portion of the top cloth. Turn the fabric and press. With glue, fasten the loose edge of the top piece over the eyes and glue the side edges to the wood. Attach bottom piece in the same way.

To make the gator with gaping eyes, get a piece of $\frac{1}{2}$-inch wood 4 inches wide and 27 inches long, two $1\frac{1}{2}$-inch-diameter round wooden drawer pulls, 5 inches of $\frac{1}{2}$-inch dowel, two hinges, nontoxic paint, and $\frac{1}{2}$ yard of corduroy. For the gator's head, cut two 13-inch lengths of plywood and save the 1-inch piece left over. Cut a notch $\frac{5}{8}$ inch wide and 5 inches long along both edges of each board to form the snout and jaws. Join the larger ends with two hinges; paint and set aside to dry.

Next, cut the dowel into 10 segments, $\frac{1}{2}$ inch long, for teeth. Glue six teeth to the upper jaw and four to the lower jaw as shown in the photograph. For nostrils, cut a $2\frac{1}{2}$ by $\frac{3}{4}$-inch piece from leftover board. Drill top edges and glue the straight bottom side to the end of the snout. Make the eyes as described for the frog. Using the alligator pattern, assemble the alligator's neck and body as described for the frog. Glue the neck to the head about $4\frac{1}{2}$ inches from the hinges.

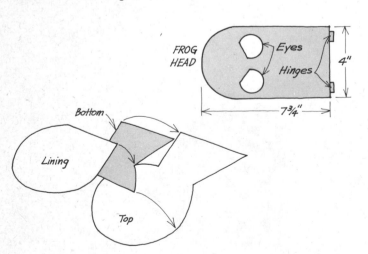

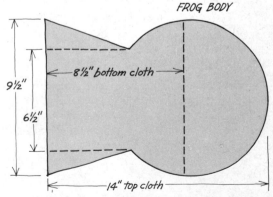

FROG HEAD AND BODY are cut following pattern above. Cut two pieces of wood for head; top and bottom cloth for body.

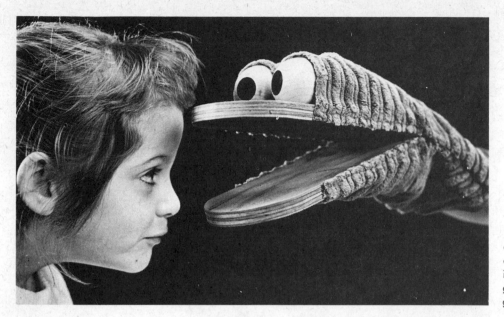

FROG with bulging eyes is made of wood and corduroy, cut according to the drawings on facing page and assembled with glue. His eyes are drawer pulls glued to the top of the head.

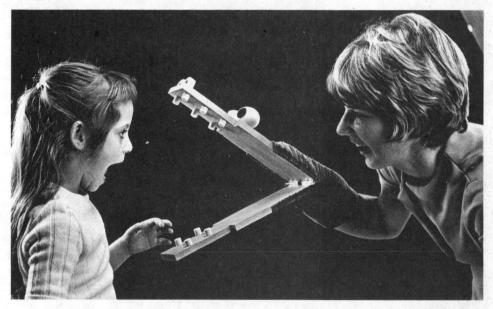

SCARY ALLIGATOR has dowels glued to inside of hinged mouth for teeth. Cut two wooden head pieces and two pieces of cloth (see drawings below).

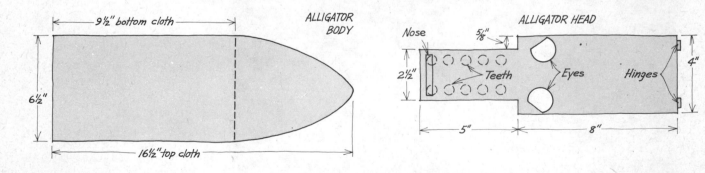

ALLIGATOR BODY

9½" bottom cloth

6½"

16½" top cloth

ALLIGATOR HEAD

Nose

5/8"

2½"

Teeth

Eyes

Hinges

4"

5"

8"

Socks Make Fine Puppets

Even very young children can manipulate these sock puppets. They slide over the hand like a glove, and with the fingers above the mouth and the thumb below it, the puppets can be made to talk. It takes about an hour to make one of the puppets. For each you'll need a sock—try a variety of sizes and colors. You'll also need some scraps of fabric, felt, and yarn; miscellaneous buttons and trimmings; and some absorbent cotton for stuffing.

First, make the puppet's mouth. Except for size and location, it is the same for both animal and people puppets. To make an animal's mouth, cut a slit around the toe of the sock, starting at the point where the lower joint of the big toe would be and continuing around to the lower joint of the little toe. The people puppet's mouth is on the side of the sock opposite the heel, about halfway between the heel and toe. Cut a slit about 2 to 2½ inches deep through the double thickness (the slit will be 4 to 5 inches wide).

For each puppet, cut from felt two U-shaped mouth pieces the width of the slit and 2 to 3½ inches long; a tongue; two sets of teeth (if desired), each in a long strip the width of the slit with scallops along one edge. To insert the mouth, turn the sock inside out. Pin strips of teeth (with scalloped edges inside) to the top and bottom of the slit and machine stitch. Next, pin the right sides of the U-shaped mouth pieces together and insert the tongue between them. Machine stitch the tongue in place across the straight edge. Pin right sides of the mouth and sock together and machine stitch the oval. Turn the sock right side out.

Give the puppets personality by adding hair, hats, eyes, and other features. To make hair and manes, cut about 20 pieces of yarn, double the length you want the hair to be. Place the pieces parallel to each other and machine stitch back and forth down the center of the head. For hats, try a bandana made from a triangular piece of fabric, a barrette cut from a circle of felt, or make a felt crown. Eyes and noses can be made with buttons, felt, yarn, or ball fringe. For each ear, cut two pieces of felt in the same shape but with one at least ½ inch smaller than the other. Place the smallest on top and sew the two together down the center; fold in half lengthwise and sew across the bottom edge. Hand-sew the ears to the puppet's head. Earrings are curtain hanger rings, clamped to the side of the puppet's head. Beards and mustaches are made by sewing on clothing cotton. To make clothing for the people puppets, cut a hole in a rectangular piece of fabric. Sew by hand around the puppet's neck and attach felt hands if desired. If a small child will be using an animal puppet made from an adult-sized sock, stuff absorbent cotton into the nose. Stuff cotton into the people puppet's head.

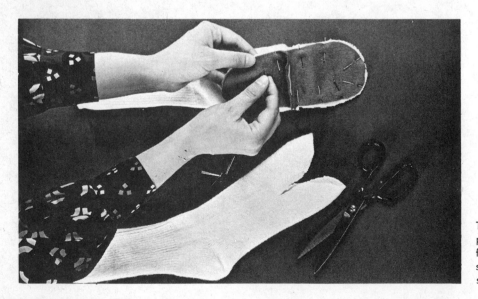

TO MAKE A MOUTH for an animal puppet, cut around toe of sock, pin felt mouth pieces and tongue (if desired) in place, stitch. Sew in teeth—scalloped strips of felt.

The Pop Puppet

If your child likes novelty toys, this cross between a puppet and a jack-in-the-box is it. The pop puppet pops up from his cone when the child pushes the dowel, then folds back down when the dowel is pulled. To make him you'll need bendable cardboard for the cone, a 15-inch-long ³⁄₁₆-inch dowel, and two round wooden cabinet pulls—one 1¹⁄₂ inches in diameter for the head, the other 2 inches in diameter for the handle. (If you prefer, use cork balls.) Drill a hole in each ball in which to insert the dowel.

To make the pop puppet, draw a quarter circle with a 7¹⁄₂-inch radius onto a piece of cardboard, then cut it out. Using the cardboard as a pattern, cut out a cloth cover large enough to fold over about 1 inch along the curved edge and ¹⁄₂ inch along the straight edges. Glue the fabric to the cardboard, slashing the curved edge so it will lie flat and wrapping excess material around the edges. Let the glue dry.

For the puppet's body, follow the pattern in the drawing, cutting two identical pieces of fabric and two felt hands. Pin the hands to the ends of the arms with the fingers pointing inwards. Pin the body pieces together (the hands inside) and stitch along the sides, arms, and top, leaving a ¹⁄₄-inch hole at the neck. Turn the fabric right side out, then press the raw, bottom edge under about ¹⁄₂ inch.

Roll the fabric-covered cardboard into a cone, overlapping the edges about ³⁄₄-inch. Glue and clamp with rubber bands and paper clips until dry. When dry, reinforce the seam with thread, using an overcast stitch and a curved needle. Insert a ³⁄₁₆-inch dowel through the cone and body. Hand stitch the neck tightly around the dowel and glue it, allowing about ¹⁄₂ inch of the dowel to protrude.

Paint a face and glue yarn hair onto the 1¹⁄₂-inch ball and attach it to the dowel with glue. Glue the 2-inch ball to the other end of the dowel. Sew the lower edge of the body to the rim of the cone.

PUPPET OR JACK-IN-THE-BOX? Pop puppet lives in a cone (above). When the dowel is all the way down, he's invisible, but push up and he peeps over the edge or jumps into full view. Photograph below shows construction details.

Yarn hair
1½" wooden ball
Glue neck to dowel
Stitch hands into seam
Stitch doll body to cone
Cloth glued to cone
³⁄₁₆" dowel
2" cork or wood ball

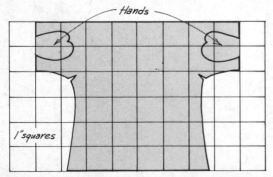

Hands

1"squares

FOLLOW PATTERN above (1-inch grids) and cut two pieces of fabric. Sew wrong sides together, hands facing inwards.

For Staging a Show

Curtain up! This puppet theater can be made out of lightweight foam-core board (a layer of foam sandwiched between two layers of poster board). The advantages of foam-core board are that it is inexpensive, lightweight, and can be cut with a razor blade or mat knife. The board is available at art and craft supply stores.

Cut 1 foot off the height of two 40 by 60-inch foam-core boards, using a straight edge and mat knife or razor blade. Cut one of the boards in half lengthwise to form the side flaps. Place an 18 by 24-inch straight-sided pine picture frame 6 inches from the top of the uncut board, equidistant from the sides, and trace around it; cut out this rectangle.

To make the hinges as shown in the drawings, you'll need two rolls of 1½-inch fabric tape. To cover the theater, buy at least 8 yards of adhesive-backed plastic (patterned material requires more for matching). Bring the plastic flush with the hinged edges and lap it over onto the inside along the outer edges and front opening.

Cut two notches, ½ inch from each end, in a 41-inch-long 1 by 2. Each notch should be ¼ inch wide. Paint the bar and the picture frame. When the frame is dry, attach eye screws (large enough to fit snugly around a ⅜-inch dowel) at upper corners of the frame. Insert the frame into the front opening and, if necessary, secure with tape on the inside.

For the curtains, cut ¾ yard of fabric into two 18 by 26-inch pieces. Stitch ¼-inch hems along the longer side edges. Along the top of the curtains make a 1-inch casing, hemming the bottom edges. Thread a 25-inch-long ⅜-inch dowel through the casings; position the ends in the eyescrews; tie back the curtains. The backdrop of the stage (1⅔ yards of dark fabric) is similar to the curtains except that it is uncut and the casing is 3 inches wide. Thread the support bar through the casing and position about halfway back.

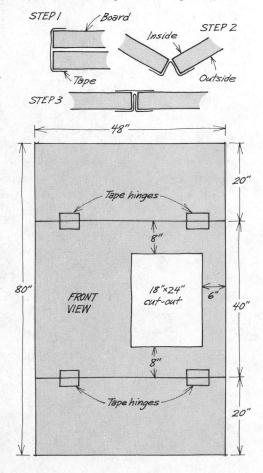

CHILDREN ARE FASCINATED when puppets talk and move from inside a theater. Cut, assemble foam-core boards as shown in drawings.

SEE FACING PAGE FOR INSTRUCTIONS

Play Yard Ideas

Back Yard Play Structure

The elements in this play yard are designed to appeal to many ages at the same time. Here are things to clamber over, under, and through; swings; and a slide. A central feature of the play yard is an 8-foot-high tower. A slide, leading from the tower's lower level, is 3 feet off the ground. A ladder leads to the second level. Two ladders attached to the structure provide vertical and horizontal climbing and also support a swing.

A wooden flag pole set in concrete goes up through a hole cut in the first level of the tower; this serves as a fireman's pole for sliding to the ground or for shinnying up to the structure. At one side of the play structure, blocks of 6 by 6s cut to different lengths are set securely in the ground, making an ideal climbing tower for young children. Bark chips cover the entire play yard and cushion jumps and falls.

ELEMENTS OF STRUCTURE at left include a wooden flag pole set in concrete for sliding down (above), climbing ladders and a swing (below left), blocks of 6 by 6s for climbing (below right).

A Children's Back Yard

Swings, slides, climbing ladders, and chinning bars are standard elements of a play yard. Here they are incorporated into a single play yard, but you could easily use the ideas individually.

The center of the play yard is divided into two sections: one of sand, the other of wood chips. An A-frame playhouse set in the sand section has steps up one side and a tempered hardboard slide down the other. The whole unit forms an 8-foot equilateral triangle when completed.

The large climbing frame is set in the wood chip section of the play yard. The frame is supported on four 6 by 6-inch posts (each 14 feet long) set in concrete; swing-supporting cross bars are bolted near the upper ends of the posts. Two canvas swings were purchased as a set (available in sporting goods shops and toy stores); the third swing is a whirligig tire and chain that swivels on a thrust ballbearing joint. The horizontal climbing ladder is made of non-galvanized pipe. (Paint non-galvanized pipe or it will rust.) To reach the ladder, children must climb up 1¼-inch hardboard dowels driven into posts and spaced in such a way that small children are discouraged after climbing two steps.

CLIMBING AND SWINGING AREA, cushioned with wood chips, is surrounded by a concrete walk—to children, a race track. A-frame playhouse is shown on left side of photo above.

CLIMBING PEGS leading to horizontal climbing ladder are staggered to keep young children off.

SLIDE leading into sand is created by one side of the A-frame playhouse; the other side forms a ladder.

For Climbing, Swinging

Designed to look like a decorative extension of the house, this swing and play structure includes all of the climbing, swinging, and chinning devices active children enjoy. The entire structure was built against one wall of the house, which helps support one end of the swing. The same type of structure could be built in an open area of the yard by modifying the construction methods and the swing's supports.

The uprights supporting the horizontal crosspiece, the baffles, and the platform are 4 by 4s set 2½ feet in the ground. The crosspiece that holds the swing is a pair of 2 by 8s bolted to a 14-foot-long 4 by 4 upright at one end and the house at the other. Short sections of 4 by 4 are bolted between the 4 by 8s to hold the swing's ropes.

An adjustable chinning bar (1½-inch diameter iron pipe) is supported in between the platform supports. A climbing rope, hung from one end of the 4 by 8s, goes through a hole cut in the floor of the platform.

The 14-foot upright 4 by 4 at the end of the swing also helps support the screenlike, checkerboard framework of plywood panels that create a strong decorative pattern. The area beneath the structure is covered with sand.

SWING, CLIMBING PLATFORM, sliding rope, chinning bar are features of this compact play structure. It is supported by a 4 by 4 on one side, roof beam on the other.

ADJUSTABLE CHINNING BAR is fixed to two of the platform supports by U-shaped steel plates bolted to the supports.

PLAY STRUCTURE is screened from the street by plywood baffles attached to 4 by 4 supports.

Landscaped Sandbox

A sandbox can often fit neatly into an overall garden scheme. In design and construction, this sandbox is an extension of the raised planting bed next to it.

The sides are 2 by 4s stacked four high for the raised bed and three high for the sandbox. The 2 by 4s are nailed to 2 by 4 stakes. Other 2 by 4s laid flat cap the top edge, and a 2 by 4 ledge runs along the wide end of the sandbox.

Two 4 by 4 posts set in concrete support the fence that separates planting bed from sandbox and protects the plants from children, flying toys, and sand. The horizontal members are 2 by 4s. Vertical members are 1 by 2s separated by 6-inch-long 2 by 2 spacers. Treatment with preservative prolongs the life of the wooden sandbox and planting bed frame and is especially necessary if you water the plants heavily.

RAISED PLANTING BED for azaleas and sandbox were designed together; wooden screen separates them.

The Super Sandbox

The super sandbox has built-in seating and a cover that keeps sun—and even rain—from bothering children playing beneath and also forms a slidable, climbable top surface when children tire of the sand.

Two panels that form the cover are made of $3/4$-inch exterior plywood measuring 3 by 6 feet and 4 by 6 feet. They are hinged to the sunken, 2 by 8-inch wooden frame members of the sandbox.

In the down position, the panels keep out rain, leaves, and cats and make an additional play surface. Laid back flat against the ground, they act as work surfaces for sand cakes and dump trucking; close the panels and the sand slides back into the sandbox. Halfway opened, the shorter panel butts up against a cleat in the longer one, creating a cozy playhouse or a structure for climbing and sliding.

SANDBOX AND PLAYHOUSE are combined in the super sandbox. When panels are opened (bottom left) they butt together to form a playhouse inside and a slide on top. Closed (top left), they create a smooth play area.

A Barrel for Cavorting

Active children can use this barrel exerciser for running, chinning, jumping, and swinging. A child holds onto the bar for support and then runs on the barrel, adding any other cavorting he feels like. With two children on the barrel, it's a challenge to see who can control the speed.

The drum is 3 feet long and 2 feet in diameter. Its ends are circles of 3/4-inch exterior plywood; its sides are 1 by 2-inch slats nailed around the plywood circles. An old tire, cut in half and fastened over the ends with heavy brads, protects the runner from splinters. The drum rotates around a fixed, 1-inch pipe axle that is attached to two 6 by 6-inch posts. The weight is carried by 6-inch-long sections of 1 1/2-inch diameter pipe, fastened to the ends of the drum with floor plates. A ladder built onto one of the posts helps children climb aboard the barrel. The holding bar is adjustable and has caps on the ends so it can't slip out of the slots.

HOW FAST THE BARREL SPINS (above) depends on how fast the children run. Ladder helps them climb aboard. Two can run if they start at the same time. Top right: holding bar is adjustable. Bottom right: drum revolves around pipe axle through sections of pipe fastened to each end.

This Slide is Portable

Try this inexpensive, easy-to-build slide. Its width and depth let children crowd in, making it a popular plaything. To construct the slide, first attach the two rails (8-foot-long 1 by 2s) to the matt side of a 4 by 8-foot panel of ⅛-inch tempered hardboard with 4-penny nails and floor-tile adhesive or strong glue.

Build the ladder next, notching the steps for the 2 by 2 side rails. Space the steps about 12 inches apart. Secure each with six 8-penny nails and glue. Construct the front support in the same way. On its upper crosspiece, include a slanted wood block. (see drawing). Soaking is not needed to bend the hardboard, but bending it is a job for two adults. A few turns of rope around the panel will help.

Place a good quantity of strong cement on the slanted block of the front support and some along the sides of the support where they meet the hardboard. Nail through the slide's rails into the support, driving three 6-penny nails into each side of the support. Rely on the cement to hold the bottom of the chute to the top step of the ladder.

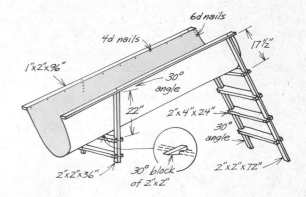

PORTABLE SLIDE can be picked up and carried to wherever the children want to play. Its deep chute is fun for children to crowd into; tall sides prevent falling out. Drawing above shows construction.

Swimming Pool Basketball

What's a good game to play in the swimming pool? How about basketball? All you need are a standard basketball ring and net, sold in sporting goods stores, and a backstop. The backstop is bolted to a 1½-inch angle-iron frame that fits the end of the diving board. The entire assembly clamps onto the diving board with two C-clamps.

BACKSTOP AND BASKET just clamp onto the diving board with C-clamps. Angle iron frame has a right-angle shape. Build the frame to fit the width of the diving board.

Basketball Backstop

Basketball players of any size can use this adjustable-height basket. The backstop is secured at the height you want (from the regulation 10 feet on down) by a pair of latches on the posts. Construction is shown in the drawing. Materials include fir or similar lumber, galvanized hardware, and a regulation hoop and net, sold in sporting goods stores and some hardware stores.

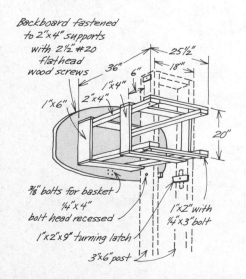

Backboard fastened to 2"x4" supports with 2½" #20 flathead wood screws
25½"
36"
6"
18"
1"x4"
2"x4"
1"x6"
20"
⅜" bolts for basket
¼"x4" bolt head recessed
1"x2" with ¼"x3" bolt
1"x2"x9" turning latch
3"x6" post

BACKSTOP ADJUSTS to low levels for shorter players, goes up the posts to the standard 10 feet for tall ones. Drawing at left shows construction.

This Hawk is a Kite

An exciting variation of traditional two and three-stick kites, this hawk kite is made of rattan or split bamboo and tissue paper—both available at craft and hobby stores.

First make the wings by bending and tying together the ends of two equal lengths of split bamboo or rattan with string. Tie the ends of a third piece together into a teardrop shape for the kite's body. Next, tie the body to the wings, separating the wings to give the kite more surface area. Reinforce all string-tied joints with white glue.

When the frame is completed, trace its outline onto tissue or rice paper, then cut out the paper slightly larger than the outline. Glue the paper to frame, folding the edges under. Decorate the side of the paper opposite the frame.

To finish the kite, tie a string between the wing tips, bending them into a bow. Make a three-leg string bridle: one string should be tied to the top of each wing equidistant from the center of the kite; the third string is tied to the bottom of the kite. The loose ends of the three strings are tied together. Add a cloth tail, 12 to 15 feet long.

If you have trouble flying the kite, a review of kiting fundamentals might be helpful. The kite string and bridle should hold the kite into the wind at approximately a 45° angle. Air blowing against the kite's surface is redirected downwards, forming an upwards push and a partial vacuum behind and above the kite. If these pressures are stronger than the kite's weight, the kite will rise.

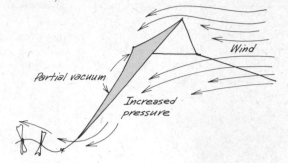

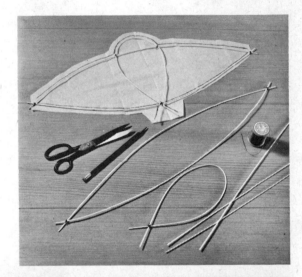

BEND AND TIE bamboo or 1/16-inch dowels for frame (top right), cover with paper (bottom right), and add bridle (below).

A Giant Rocking Giraffe

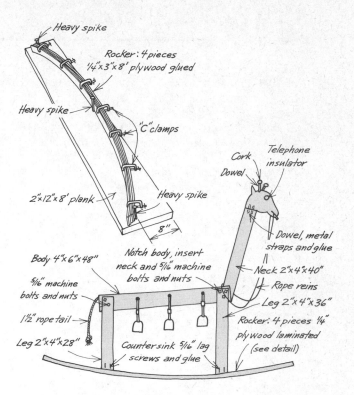

Here's a 7-foot-high rocking giraffe—a toy big enough for three children to use at once. The giraffe is a sawhorse mounted on rockers with a head cut from a block of redwood and attached to a 2 by 4 by 40-inch neck. He was painted brown and yellow and given a coat of clear acrylic spray.

The drawing shows construction of the head and body. To make each rocker, laminate four strips of 1/4-inch exterior plywood, 3 inches wide by 8 feet long, with slow-drying resin glue. While the glue is still soft, place each rocker in the shaping device shown in the drawing, clamping the strips together until the glue is dry. When the glue hardens, the rockers retain their curve. The ends will be staggered as a result of the curving and can be trimmed off. Instead of clamps, you could use wire to hold the strips.

If you use this shaping device and want the two rockers to have identical curves, pencil the outline of the first rocker on the face of the 2 by 12 shaping board. If the second rocker doesn't follow the curve exactly, make any necessary adjustments by driving in some additional nails. These rockers have a curve of about 8 inches in 8 feet. You can vary the curve by whatever amount you wish. If the curve is too sharp, however, the giraffe may be too wild.

THREE CHILDREN can ride the giant rocking giraffe, right. Construction is detailed in the drawings (top of page). Bend the laminated rockers in the form shown in the drawing. The head (above) is cut from a block of redwood and fastened to the neck by dowels and metal straps; cover joint with plastic wood filler. Stirrups are circles or squares of 3/4-inch plywood with the centers cut out.

Triangles for Building

Four 4 by 8-foot sheets of plywood can be turned into 20 equilateral triangles for making anything from tepees to moon ships. Cut the triangles as shown in the drawing, then cut 15-inch diameter holes in some of them. Cut seven 3-inch holes in other triangles with a saber saw or hole bit in a drill. Keep the holes within a 15-inch circle so they won't weaken the edges.

Connect four or five groups of three triangles each with hinges (see drawing) to make assembling the shapes in various ways easiest. Along the outer edges of the hinged sections and the other triangles, drill 5/8-inch holes, 1 inch in, so they can be tied together.

DRAWING AT LEFT shows how to cut plywood for toy above.

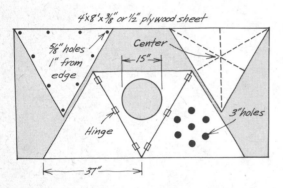

A "Real" Locomotive

Built for a 3-year-old, this locomotive can't highball down the sidewalk because the wheels are fixed to the frame, but it still makes a great rocking, climbing, and pretending toy.

Various materials were used for the locomotive, including a 12-inch-diameter furnace pipe for the boiler and an empty paint can for the smokestack. The frame is two 5-foot-long 2 by 4s braced apart by three 16-inch-long 2 by 4s. The other parts—cab, wheels, and cowcatcher—are made of 1 by 12 and 1 by 10-inch lumber. Construction is shown in the drawings.

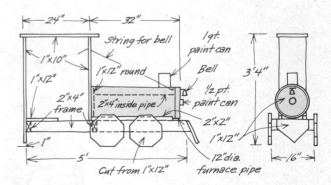

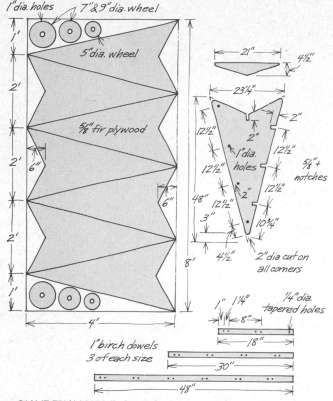

Diagram labels:
- 1" dia. holes
- 7" & 9" dia. wheel
- 5" dia. wheel
- 5/8 fir plywood
- 1'
- 2'
- 2'
- 2'
- 1'
- 6"
- 6"
- 4'
- 8'
- 21"
- 4½"
- 23¼"
- 2"
- 2"
- 12½"
- 12½"
- 1" dia. holes
- 12½"
- 12½"
- 2"
- 12½"
- 5/8" + notches
- 48"
- 3"
- 10¾"
- 4½"
- 2" dia cut on all corners
- 1" 1¼"
- 8"
- ¼" dia. tapered holes
- 18"
- 1" birch dowels 3 of each size
- 30"
- 48"

GIANT TRIANGLES (below left, right), cut from a sheet of 5/8-inch plywood, dowels, and plywood circles as shown in above drawing, can be assembled into ships, cars, and jungle gyms.

Plywood Building Toy

Building and creating are activities that appeal to almost all children. One sheet (4 by 8 feet) of 5/8-inch plywood can be cut into the 14 triangles and 6 wheels that are the basic parts of this giant building toy; add 1-inch hardwood dowels and you have all the elements for creating forts, jungle gyms, and boats.

Follow the diagram and cut out the seven large triangles and seven smaller ones. Cut six wheels (two each with 5, 7, and 9 inch diameters) from the scraps.

Next, cut the four 5/8-inch notches in each of the large triangles. Drill a hole in the center of each wheel and drill four holes along the side of each large triangle to fit the 1-inch dowels. (You might want to ream the holes slightly larger than 1 inch so the dowels will fit through them easily.)

Cut the 1-inch dowels to the lengths indicated in the diagram. Cut a number of ¼-inch dowel pins, 1½ inches long, and drill ¼-inch tapered holes in the 1-inch dowels to fit the pins. Sand all the parts of the building toy, then finish them with nontoxic paint (optional). Wax the dowels and holes with paraffin for lubrication so assembling the toy will be easier.

Cardboard Igloo Playhouse

Materials for this playhouse can be found free at many appliance stores. You get large appliance cartons, cut them into triangles, and staple them together into a dome. First, decide how large a dome you want. Then determine its exact radius (half the distance across the dome) at the widest point. (In the dome shown here, it's at the mid-door level.) You'll need the radius to determine the two triangle sizes that make up the dome.

One triangle should have equal-length A sides, 0.6180 the length of the radius. The other triangle has one A side and two shorter B sides, 0.5465 the length of the radius. The dome shown here has a 40-inch radius; thus its triangles have A sides that are 24$\frac{23}{32}$ inches long and B sides that are 21$\frac{7}{8}$ inches long. Mark off these lengths on two pieces of wood lath, drilling a small nail hole at one of the marks and a pen-sized hole at the other.

To make a triangle, draw the common A-length base along a yardstick. With one lath, draw arcs while holding the nail on the ends of the base line. Then draw straight lines from the arc intersection to the ends of the base line. Add 1-inch-wide cut lines around the triangle; cut it out with a mat knife and lightly score the inside lines. Fold up the flaps along the scored line. You'll need 15 triangles with all A sides and 45 triangles with one A side and two shorter B sides. Assemble the smaller AB triangles into 6 pentagons and 5 three-triangle semipentagons, as shown in the drawing, stapling the B sides together and leaving the A sides on the perimeter. Finish the dome (see drawings). Fill in around the bottom with five thin triangles having two B sides and a base long enough to fill the gaps beneath the semipentagons. Tack the bottom flaps of the finished dome to a plywood base.

DOME-SHAPED PLAYHOUSE is made of triangles cut from cardboard boxes.

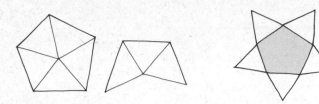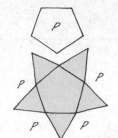

FIRST STAPLE AB triangles into 6 pentagons, 5 semipentagons. Add A triangles to perimeter of one pentagon. Fill gaps between triangles with other pentagons (P). Add A triangles between and below pentagons, then add semipentagons at bottom.

DRAW ARCS with laths, then connect intersections with straight lines for folding. Draw cut lines 1 inch out.

FOLD TRIANGLES along inner fold line, then staple them together as shown in the drawings above.

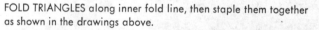

THIN TRIANGLES, cut to fit, fill the bottom of the completed dome, shown upside down in above photograph.

INSIDE THE PLAYHOUSE, the stapled flaps of the triangles are visible. Nail bottom of playhouse to wooden boards.

Portable Playhouse

You'll appreciate this playhouse. It is made from 2 by 2s bolted together with wing nuts and covered with tie-on canvas panels and is particularly easy to assemble and dismantle. The design calls for about 22 yards of canvas 31 inches wide. (For different fabric widths, either change the amount of material in the hems or shorten the 2 by 2s so two widths of seamed fabric will span the large panels.) Turn the canvas back an inch or less for hems all around; sew on 20-inch ties about every 13 inches, starting 5 inches from the corners. Five-eighths-inch cotton awning binding (about 76 yards) from an awning store or any strong tape will do.

For the wooden frame, you'll need 128 feet of common fir 2 by 2s: nine 10-foot, four 8-foot, and one 6-foot length. Cut one 53-inch piece, five 54-inch pieces, nine 60-inch pieces, two 73½-inch pieces, two 96-inch, and two 112-inch pieces. Mark key pieces with letters as in the diagram for easy assembly (for AB piece, mark an A at one end and a B at the other). Buy 32 carriage bolts (¼ by 4 inch) with washers and wing nuts to fit them.

Lay out four base pieces. Hold vertical AE inside intersection A; drill ¼-inch holes to lock securely to base pieces; install two carriage bolts. Add verticals BF, CI, and DJ in the same way. Drill holes in AE and BF 2 inches from the top. Drill holes in crosspiece EF about 2⅝ inches from either end and bolt to verticals to form corners E and F. Drill holes in CI and DJ, 51 inches from the bottom; affix horizontals EGK and FHL to the outside at intersections G and H and at corners E and F as in the photograph. Attach crosspiece GH on the outside of the verticals. Attach crosspiece IJ to the top. Affix EI at corner E and at I, trimming as necessary. Fit and bolt FJ similarly. Attach KL atop side horizontals, then bolt on the legs. Install a 54-inch vertical to join the midpoints of GH and CD and a 53-inch vertical to join midpoints of EF and AB. For the theater window, drill holes in AE and CI 33 inches from the bottom; attach a 60-inch piece outside.

FRAME MEMBERS of this playhouse are 2 by 2s. Walls are boldly striped canvas panels tied on. Cut 2 by 2s and assemble as shown in drawing on next page, using bolts and wing nuts.

INTERSECTION E shown from inside (left) before roof diagonal is added and from outside (right) with roof diagonal bolted on. Note how pieces are staggered one above the other to support the roof diagonal. Wing nuts should go on the inside.

INTERSECTION I (left): photograph shows how end of roof diagonal is trimmed to fit against the other members. Intersection G (right) shown from inside: two bolts hold pieces securely. Drill all holes with a ¼-inch drill bit.

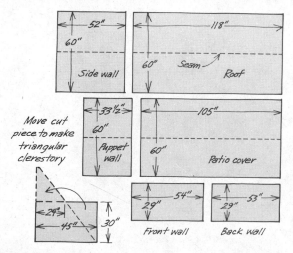

52"
60"
Side wall

118"
60"
Seam
Roof

Move cut piece to make triangular clerestory

33½"
60"
Puppet wall

105"
60"
Patio cover

24"
45"
30"

54"
29"
Front wall

53"
29"
Back wall

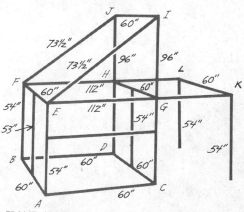

J   60"   I
73½"
73½"   96"   96"
F   H
60"   112"   60"   L   60"   K
54"
E   112"   G   54"
53"   54"
D
B
54"   60"   60"
60"   60"
A   60"   C

FRAME ASSEMBLY is shown above: letters indicate intersections. Cutting plan for fabric (left): measurements are for finished pieces. Allow 1 inch for hem allowance when figuring amount of yardage to buy.

Shoe for a Playhouse

A group of fathers built this windowed shoe playhouse for a nursery school. Though you probably won't want to undertake such a project for your own back yard, the construction features and shape might be adapted to a smaller playhouse.

The sides, floors, and roof are made of $1/2$ and $3/4$-inch exterior plywood. The framing members are 2 by 2s. The design of the playhouse provided that the shoe, 11 feet high and 18 feet long, be bolted together in sections and also be bolted to the foundation for easy assembly.

Within the shoe are various-sized rooms with connecting stairways (one spiral, one of two logs), a sliding pole, and a carpeted crawl-over. A slide, complete with waves, leads down from the upper floor rooms. Next to it is a plywood crawl-up with metal handles to assist young children. The shoe was painted before assembly in a bright color, then the trim and shutters were painted a contrasting color.

OLD MOTHER HUBBARD never had it as good as these nursery school children. Four fathers built the shoe for the school: plans allowed them to cut and paint the pieces, then assemble them on the playground (above right). You probably won't want to build a playhouse this size for your own yard but you could adapt the shape and some of the features to a smaller version. The various windows and doors would brighten any playhouse (below).

All Ages Play Here

Two stories and a tower create a playhouse that offers enough variety to challenge a crowd of children of all ages. The ground floor level is a 7 by 11-foot room built on a foundation of railway ties. The flooring is tongue and groove; the walls are sheathed in 3/8-inch exterior plywood.

The upper deck and the 7 by 8-foot clubhouse that it surrounds are supported by railway ties and reached by a ladder whose first rung is about 2½ feet high to prevent smaller children from climbing up. The lookout tower is built 4 feet above the upper deck, and a fireman's pole leading to the ground provides fast getaways.

The sturdy railings surrounding the upper deck and lookout tower are 1 by 2-inch cedar slats nailed to 2 by 3s. Hand-split cedar shakes top the plywood roof.

THREE LEVELS make this playhouse enjoyable for all ages. The clubhouse on the ground level includes windows for puppet shows and concessions stand (below). Upper levels are reached by a ladder whose first rung is too high for smaller children to reach (below right). Guard rails prevent falls.

FIREMAN'S POLE provides fast, fun exit from 3rd story lookout.

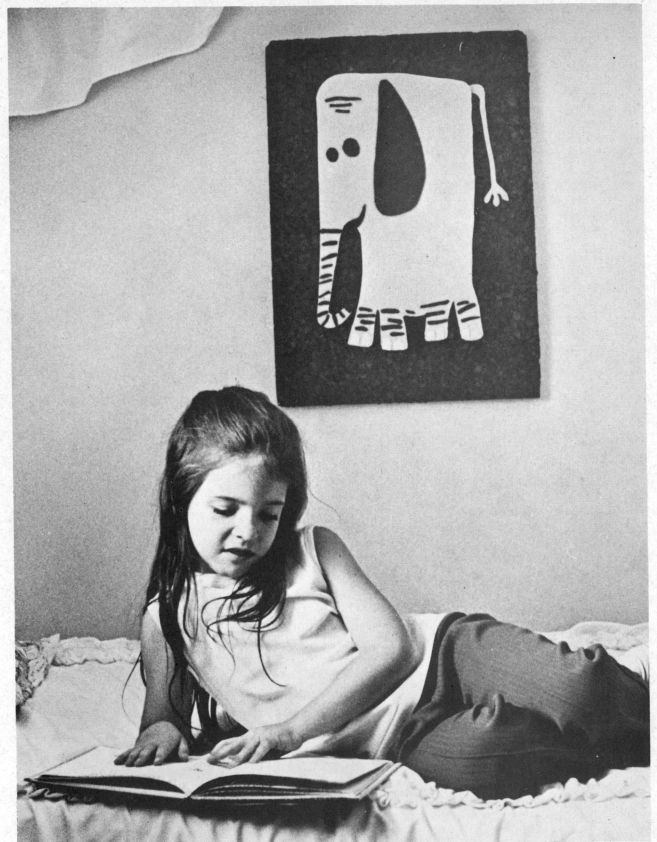

SEE FACING PAGE FOR INSTRUCTIONS

Furniture that's Fun

A Bedroom Menagerie

Stalking across a wall, these animals cut from brightly colored felt and construction paper will decorate a child's room by turning it into a menagerie of friendly beasts.

The animals in the little girl's room are cut from colored felt and pasted directly onto refrigeration cork mats with rubber cement. (Glue and paste, unless applied sparingly, will soak through and stretch the felt.) For animal ideas, look through a child's picture or coloring book.

The decorations shown in the baby's nursery were cut out of colored construction paper. By using paper folding and cutting techniques, you can make them three dimensional. The drawing is a pattern for making the elephant. For other ideas to use in making animals, look up a book on paper folding and cutting in the public library.

CARNIVAL COLORS of zoo (facing page, above), cut from felt and mounted on cork, enliven child's room.

JUNGLE ON WALL (above) was made from colorful construction paper. Three dimensional parts, such as the giraffe's and elephant's heads, were created by cutting and folding the paper. To make the elephant, use the pattern shown in the drawing at right. Children's books might offer other ideas.

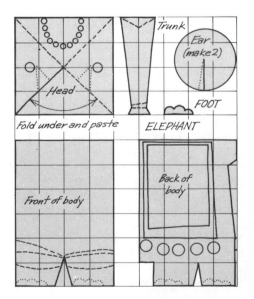

Mobile for a Nursery

Color and motion are two things that attract a young child's attention the most. This mobile has the shape of a bee and is made by covering a bent-wire frame with colorful tissue paper (available at art supply stores). The mobile can be hung from a string over the child's crib, but since the mobile is delicate, be sure to hang it out of the child's reach.

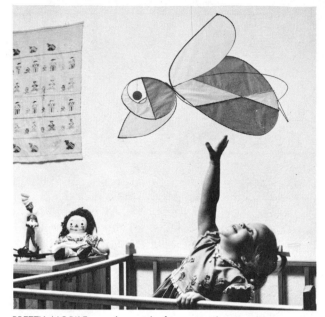

PRETTY MOBILE can be made from covering a wire or rattan frame with colorful tissue paper. This one is in the shape of a bee, but you could try any other simple shape.

GRINNING TURTLE container challenges children to return art supplies or other articles to their proper pockets. He is made of colorful burlap and felt, then hung on wall in child's room or play area.

Put a Turtle on the Wall

Children like to have this turtle grin at them as they reach for art supplies stored in pockets in his shell. He's a bit of a puzzle, too. Youngsters have to find the pocket shaped to accept paper, scissors, glue—whatever art supplies they use most.

To make the turtle, start with a rectangle of colored burlap about 20 by 30 inches. Cut the corners to make an oval for the turtle's shell. Using a zigzag stitch, sew bias tape of contrasting color to the shell along the edges of the burlap. Fold the tape around the edge of the shell when sewing, being sure to stitch down the frayed edges.

Each pair of feet is simply two rounded shapes, one smaller than the other to create the illusion of depth; cut each pair from a rectangle of felt about 8 by 15 inches. Leave enough felt at the top of each foot to be slipped under the shell and stitched to the bias tape. The head is also a piece of felt, measuring about 11 by 15 inches. Cut a rounded nose, a big grin, and a neck that is long enough to slip under the shell and be sewn. The eyes are two felt circles glued on top of two larger circles of black felt. Use colorful scraps of felt for the tail and tongue.

To make the pockets, lay out the art supplies to be stored in the shell, then cut and sew on patches of different colored felt to match each one, leaving enough slack for the supplies to slip easily in and out. Finish the turtle by sewing two loops of bias tape to the top of the shell and one loop to the head so that he can hang on a wall.

Bulletin Board Ideas

Finger paint masterpieces and pictures of friends can go on these two quite different display boards. The 6-foot-long panel bulletin board is two 2 by 3-foot cork boards framed with corner moldings that were nailed to the cork with 6-penny finishing nails. The bulletin board is suspended from wall hooks on two eyebolts.

The second display idea consists of clothespins glued to a 1 by 4-foot board that spans the window. The ends of the board are nailed to the window frame.

BOTH CURATOR AND ARTIST, this child can pin up her own artwork and prints on these two different bulletin boards. Above, she looks at a lion print clipped to a strip of plywood with a clothes-pin. The bulletin board at left is made of cork.

Animal Blackboard

An animal blackboard makes a big splash on a child's wall: several of them marching across the wall might be even more effective. For an animal like this one, you'll need a 3 by 4-foot sheet of $\frac{1}{8}$-inch tempered hardboard and blackboard paint.

Trace the outline of the animal you want onto the hardboard. Try to keep the design simple and large so it will fill most of the rectangular space on the board. Note that the front and bottom edges of this whale are the original edges of the hardboard. Use a hand keyhole saw, a saber saw, a jigsaw, or a band saw for cutting out the shapes. Save the scraps for the animal's eyes, nose, and mouth.

Blackboard paint is sold at paint stores in light green, dark green, and black. Use two coats for a durable surface. To make a bright contrast, paint the eyes and nose cutouts in yellow or another color and glue them on with white glue. If there's a shortage of wall space in the child's room, consider placing one or two of the blackboards on a fence in the play yard.

GIANT WHALE can float gracefully against a wall or a fence in the play yard. Other shapes to try are a turtle and bear.

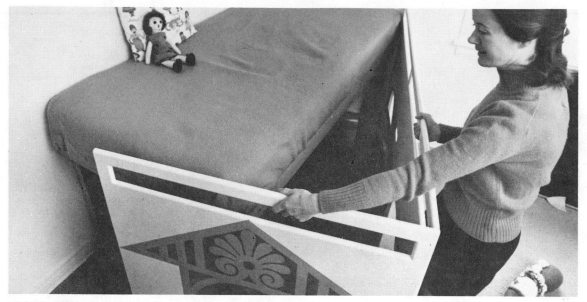

HINGED SIDES of playhouse fit around the bed frame. Barrel bolts are used to fasten it securely to frame. Guard rails at top of sides prevent falling out of bed.

This Bed is a Playhouse

Most children's rooms aren't big enough to accommodate both a bed and a playhouse. This room has them both built into one unit.

The bed is actually a table with 2 by 4 legs, 2 by 3 frame, and a ½-inch plywood top, covered with a single-bed mattress. The playhouse is created by two pieces of ¾-inch plywood, hinged together at the ends, that fit around two sides of the table-bed. The entire space inside (beneath the bed) is for play. Three small arched doors open into the play area, and inside are assorted hooks, bolts, and latches for busy play. Finger holes, drilled into the doors, serve as door handles and also make good peep holes.

A 5-inch-high railing around the top of the plywood unit keeps the child from falling off the bed. Two toe-slits cut through the plywood sides (don't cut them in the doors) make it easy for the child to climb in and out of bed.

The enclosure is painted white and the doors a bright magenta. Decorative trim is magenta and orange. The long side measures 6 feet 3 inches, the shorter one measures 3 feet 4 inches. Four barrel bolts mounted on the inside of the plywood sides hold the panels to the table-bed frame. However, there's no need to remove the enclosure for bed making or even vacuuming inside the playhouse. The playhouse is also useful as a storage place for games and toys. Doors can be cut to any size you like: enlarge them to accommodate a tricycle, make them crawl-through entries, or cut them to different sizes and shapes.

PLAYING INSIDE is fun but so is climbing on the roof. Note toe slots in side.

A Train for a Headboard

Nestled between engine and caboose, this young boy sleeps with the *Nightime Express* chugging around his bed. The plywood train bearing his initials keeps him from rolling out of bed and also makes a whimsical headboard and room decoration.

The train was first drawn onto three pieces of ½-inch plywood and then cut out. The pieces are fastened together with large dovetail joints (or use L-brackets), nails, and white glue. For extra strength, nail a 2 by 4 brace across the bottom between the sides. The sides of this headboard train are about 30 inches wide and 24 inches high. The dimensions you use will depend on the child's bed. Complete the train's details with nontoxic paint. Since the headboard is not attached to the bed, it pulls away for bedmaking.

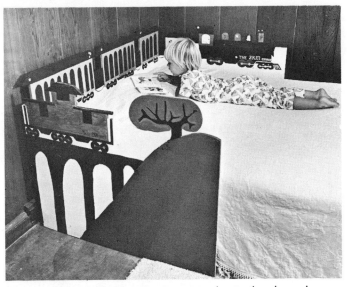

TRAIN AND LANDSCAPE outlines are traced onto the plywood, then cut out. Details are added with nontoxic paint.

ONE CUBE can be a sturdy desk with a hole for the child's feet. In a moment, all three cubes become a hiding place, mountain, playhouse, or submarine (bottom photograph).

Plywood Cubes for Fun

These cubes stack, store, and have all sorts of practical uses. They also make great oversized blocks to create imaginary mountains, rooms, castles, and holes to climb in and out of.

You can make three cubes from a 4 by 8-foot sheet of ½-inch plywood. Each side of a finished cube measures 16 inches square. Cut the top and bottom pieces 16 inches square, two of the sides 16 by 15 inches, and the other two sides 15 by 15 inches.

Assemble the cubes as shown in the drawing, using glue and 1-penny finishing nails to hold the simple butt joints. Cut a 12-inch hole in one side of each cube with a saber saw or keyhole saw. (For added play possibilities, you might cut two holes in one of the cubes.) Puttying and sanding all corners, edges, and joints will improve the cubes' appearance, as well as reduce splintering. The cubes shown here were painted white on the outside and bright colors inside.

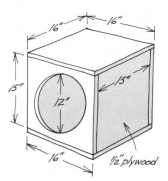

A Child-size Lounge

Here is a delightful lounge for children. It is scaled to their size and built for their reading, resting, and romping. The wood framing of the couch is easy to build with few tools, and its upholstering involves one of the easiest techniques.

To build the couch, first cut the two ends out of ³/₄-inch plywood to approximately the shape shown in the drawing. Then cut the two 2 by 2s and two 1 by 7¹/₂-inch pieces of clear fir to 52¹/₂ inches and attach them to the plywood ends with white glue and screws. The 1 by 7¹/₂-inch pieces should be a full 1 inch thick (not ³/₄ inch). Cut a shelf for toys out of ¹/₈-inch hardboard or ¹/₄-inch plywood and attach it to the 2 by 2s with white glue and small nails.

For upholstery you'll need a 54-inch length of 8-inch cylindrical polyurethane foam and 10 feet of 30-inch-wide heavy upholsterer's burlap (both available at upholstery shops). Cut the foam in half lengthwise with a serrated bread knife and glue the two halves to the 1 by 7¹/₂-inch members with rubber cement. The foam will be slightly overlong, so tuck the ends up to give extra padding on the lounge's ends.

Cover the plywood ends with the upholstery fabric of your choice (you'll need 3¹/₂ yards of 60-inch-wide fabric), using tacks or a staple gun to affix it to the insides of the plywood ends. Cut and sew the burlap together to make one piece to cover the front, seat, seat back, and top (but not the open back, as shown). Overlap and double-stitch the seams for strength. Tack the burlap along the top edge of the back first, then tack it down the sides, stretching it as tight as you can and turning the edges under. Keep the tacks on the inner edges of the plywood ends to leave room for ornamental upholstery tacks.

Sew hook-and-pile tape to the two sides of the part of the upholstery fabric that will hang down to enclose the back of the lounge. Staple or tack the matching strip to the back edges of the ends. Then stretch and tack on the upholstery fabric over the burlap, again turning edges under and applying ornamental upholstery tacks about 1 inch apart.

COLORFUL UPHOLSTERY makes lounge a plaything as well as a piece of furniture.

LOUNGE'S FRAME is made as shown below with 3/4-inch plywood, 2 by 2s, hardboard, and 1 by 7½-inch fir. Fir boards should be a full 1 inch thick for strength, not 3/4 inch.

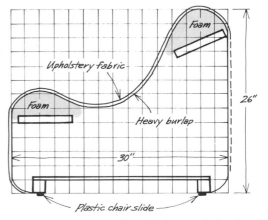

CROSS SECTION (2-inch grid) shows upholstering. Only the upholstery fabric (not underlining) extends down back.

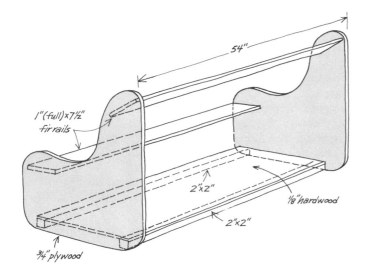

JUST RIGHT FOR CHILDREN, this lounge is comfortable, inexpensive, and not difficult to make. Colorfully printed upholstery fabric hangs down in the back to hide a storage shelf for toys underneath.

Table for Crafts and Ping Pong

You'll appreciate this table—so versatile it's almost constantly in use for games of all types, for crafts, and for studying. When folded, the top surface (two hollow-core doors) is 2 by 7 feet. An 8-inch overhang on one side of the top leaves leg room for sitting. When unfolded, the table is 4 by 7 feet—large enough for a ping-pong table. Plenty of room for storage is provided by shelves below the table top; plastic dish pans are used as bins for games and craft supplies.

Shelves, dividers, and sides are built from ³/₄-inch plywood. The top and bottom frames are 2 by 2s. Thin wood stripping is used to cover the plywood edges. The swingout legs, made from 2 by 2s, swing on standard door hinges.

Between the two 24-inch-wide hollow-core doors, which act as the work top, is a piano hinge that runs the length of the doors—7 feet. A plastic laminate protects the edges of both doors and the work surface of the door on top when folded. The open table could also be covered if a protected surface is desired.

For a fully opened table, the side legs swing out for the top to rest on. To make a ping-pong table, lay a sheet of ¹/₄-inch tempered hardwood on top. Cut the board into quarters and hinge them together with heavy cloth tape for easy storage.

HOLLOW CORE DOORS, hinged down the center, form the top of the table. For crafts and games, doors fold together, one on top of the other. Plastic laminate on surfaces and edges of doors makes cleaning up after play easy.

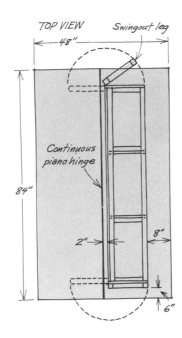

TOP VIEW — Swingout leg

48"

Continuous piano hinge

84"

2" 8"

6"

HARDBOARD SURFACE, cut into four sections and hinged back together, fits on top of the table for ping pong.

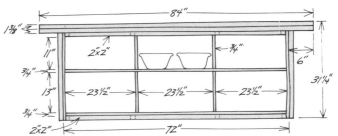

84"

1¾"

11"

2x2

¾"

6"

¾"

13"

23½" 23½" 23½"

31¼"

¾"

2x2

72"

END VIEW (closed)

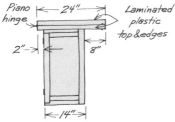

Piano hinge

24"

Laminated plastic top & edges

2" 8"

14"

END VIEW (open)

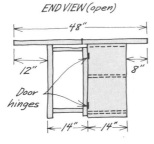

48"

12" 8"

Door hinges

14" 14"

LEGS ON EITHER SIDE of the frame swing out (see drawings) to support the unfolded top. An overhang allows leg room when table is folded.

SEE INSTRUCTIONS ON FACING PAGE

Parties and Holidays

Instead of a Mask

Becoming something or someone else is one of the things children enjoy most about Halloween. And with a little help they can assemble a simple make-up kit that will transform them into as convincing a clown or ghoul as you'd ever expect. (Make-up is also safer than a mask because it won't slip to block vision.)

Younger children will need adult help in making themselves up; older ones will probably like to put it on each other or, with the help of a small stand-up mirror, will like to dress themselves up.

You may already have cold cream, eyebrow pencils, lipstick, powder, and rouge. For more colors and unusual effects, visit a theatrical make-up store. (Look under "Theatrical Supplies" and "Theatrical Make-up" in the yellow pages of the phone directory.) Add-ons such as big noses, clear glasses, and mustaches can be found in a costume or joke store.

Caution: If you're worried that a child's skin might be sensitive to make-up, you should buy hypoallergenic cosmetics at department stores or pharmacies. Be careful at all times to keep make-up from getting too close to the eyes and mouth. Help younger children when they're working in these areas.

Theatrical make-up is applied in much the same way as cosmetic make-up but with exaggerated results. First, cover the skin completely with a thin layer of cold cream. Its smooth surface makes application and removal of the make-up easier. Remove excess cream. Next, apply a base make-up (sometimes called pancake) with a small sponge. It comes in many colors. Professional actors usually pat on a loose translucent powder as a sealer. If the powder mutes the colors underneath, add more color on top.

For large patches of color, make streaks on the face with grease paint sticks, then carefully blend the streaks together with your fingertips. Use a soft eyebrow pencil or make-up crayon for linework.

To remove make-up, dab on large amounts of cold cream and gently wipe off the color with tissue paper. When most of it is removed, wash with soap and water.

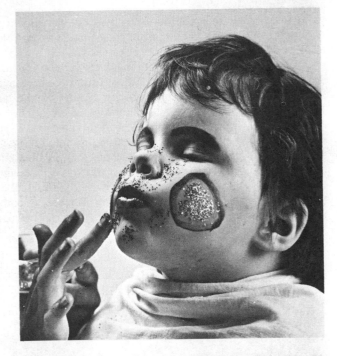

CLOWNS, RACCOONS, HOBOS, GOBLINS are all possible with theatrical make-up that is safe, easy to use, and won't block vision. Add-ons include noses, glasses, moustaches, glitter.

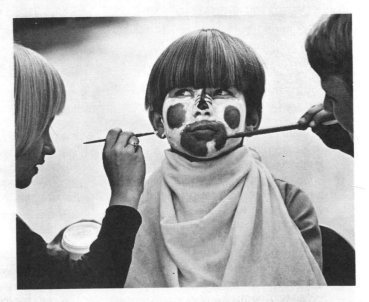

Paper Bag Costumes

Giant paper bags are what these costumes really are. You make them from one sheet of paper in minutes. They cost almost nothing. And even a very young child can decorate his own. To make a paper bag costume, you'll need a 36 by 52-inch sheet of heavy brown wrapping paper. (You may need to adjust this size to fit your child—these fit 6 to 10-year-olds with ease.)

Fold the paper into a roll, short side to short side, and glue a 2-inch overlap. Fold the roll to a bag shape: 15 inches across both front and back and 10 inches to each side, with side centerfolds as in standard brown paper bags. To avoid undue stress, plan folding so that the seam is not along a side.

Animal ears are made by measuring a 4-inch square at both top corners. Make slits down 4 inches from the top, then cut out the center section. Fold all the cut edges to the inside to form perky, triangular, stand-up ears. Glue along the top edge to close the head.

Arm holes are an oval shape, measuring about 4 by 12 inches in both side sections. The bottom of the holes start about 7 inches from the bottom of the bag or where comfortable. Add reinforcement with cellophane tape to prevent rips and tears.

Try the bag on the child to determine where eye holes should be placed. These start about 7 inches down from the top of the head on the mask. Be sure to cut the eye holes large enough so that if the bag shifts while on the child, he will still be able to see. The heartlike shape of these eyeholes gives almost enough room for all of the child's face to be seen. Animal details made with colored paper are the final touches. Cut them to size and glue on.

Caution: The bag limits the child's vision. Plan to attach some reflective tape to the costumes or decorate them with fluorescent paint so they can be seen easily by passing motorists. You might want to accompany smaller children on trick or treat outings.

EVEN THE MOST HORRIBLE looking monster becomes docile when he says, "Trick or treat." These spooks are just heavy wrapping paper.

A Mask for Everyone

A Halloween mask-making project will capture the imagination of most children. For their masks, the children used simple materials ranging from paper plates to empty ice cream containers. With a little paint, paper, and glue, you have enough material to create the kinds of creatures children like.

For a papier mâché mask, first blow up a large balloon (4-inch diameter when flat). Dip paper strips in liquid starch and pat about four layers of them onto the balloon. When dry, remove the balloon, draw on eyes, nose, and mouth, then cut them out with a mat knife. Paint on facial details. Cut off enough from the bottom for the child's head to fit through.

A paper plate can become a simple mask. Stretch brightly colored burlap around a dinner-sized paper plate and staple the edges. Cut out eye and nose holes, and add face details cut from colored construction paper. To hold the mask on, staple the ends of a strip of elastic (sold in farbic stores) to the sides of the plate.

Ice cream containers that are often available from ice cream shops make fine masks. Mark eye holes on a clean 3-gallon ice cream carton and cut them out. Use poster paint and construction paper to create any face the child wants.

Simple masks can be made out of construction paper. Fold a piece of heavy colored paper in half. Draw in eyes, nose and mouth, then cut them out with scissors. Round the corners of the folded paper to make a face shape. Add whiskers, ears, eyebrows, and anything else that's fun—cut from colored paper. Attach an elastic band to the mask to hold it on.

SIMPLE MATERIALS were used to make all of the masks shown here. Above (clockwise from top): papier mâché molded over a balloon with coat hanger antennae; rabbit mask made from folded construction paper; paper plate mask and paper hat. Below (left to right): two masks made from ice cream containers and a rabbit created by covering a balloon with papier mâché. Details are created with paper and paint.

Party Games

For a neighborhood penny carnival, a birthday party, or just to keep a group of children busy, here are games, contests, and ideas for getting a children's party rolling.

Along with the ideas illustrated in the photographs, you might like to try the following games. Fishing is a long-time favorite. Find the biggest box you can or pile two large open boxes on top of each other. Make a fishing pole, line, and "hook" from a stick, string, and a clothespin. You or one of the children crouch inside the box and attach a prize of candy or a small toy to the clothespin each time a child passes the pole over. Every child catches a "fish."

For a peanut pitching game, each contestant stands behind a line and tosses peanuts at a bucket or dish. He wins if the peanut lands inside.

A test for young marksmen is blasting away at a lighted candle with a water pistol. The child who puts out the flame in the least amount of time wins. (Supervise this contest closely.)

A popular party refreshment for a warm afternoon is snow cones. Just fill paper cups with crushed or shaved ice and add fruit punch concentrate. Serve snow cones with a straw and spoon.

SHAVING A BALLOON (below) is tricky—even trickier when you're being timed. Fastest shaver wins this contest. In right photo, children toss water-filled balloons at nails in board.

COOKY DECORATING is fun. Use ready-to-spread frosting.

MAKING NECKLACES from dyed macaroni keeps children busy.

AERONAUTICS TEST: children fold and toss paper planes at hoop.

Have a Piñata Party

An exciting party idea from Mexico in which *all* the children win a prize is the piñata. When a blindfolded youngster hits the swinging and bobbing piñata with a bat, it breaks, spilling out candy and small toys that the children scramble for.

In Mexico, the core of the piñata is an olla, or clay pot. Exported versions of the piñata found in import and variety stores are made of heavy paper or cardboard. The piñatas shown here are formed around balloons, and are inexpensive and easy to make.

Blow up a balloon and place it in a bowl to keep it from shifting. Cover the balloon with about two thicknesses of newspaper strips dipped in starch. Leave a small area by the tied end uncovered to make an opening for putting in presents and goodies.

In a couple of days, when the paper has hardened and dried, punch holes around the opening for wire or string from which to hang the piñata. Pop the balloon and remove it through the opening.

You can decorate the piñata with cardboard, paint, and tissue paper. Fill it with small items (enough for all of the children) that will tolerate the fall to the ground. To befuddle the already blindfolded batsman, hang the piñata from a pulley over a tree limb or rafter so that it can be pulled up and down as the children swing. Give each child three swings with the bat.

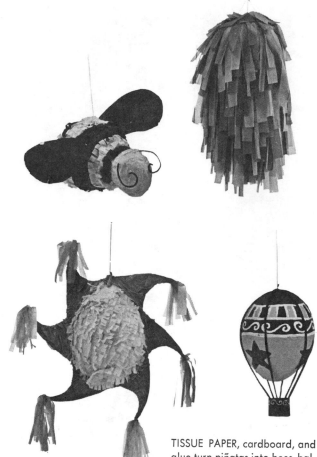

TISSUE PAPER, cardboard, and glue turn piñatas into bees, balloons, and other shapes.

SHOWER OF GOODIES will rain down on these children if the batsman connects with the swinging and bobbing piñata. Fill the piñata with enough prizes for all the children.

STARCH-SOAKED STRIPS of newspaper wrapped around a balloon forms the core of the piñatas shown above. Paint, colorful tissue paper, and cardboard create details.

The Lollipop Tree

Why shouldn't a swing-out tree that holds lollipops delight children? It's easy to construct and it folds flat for storage between holidays.

The tree is a series of 1 by 1s that pivot around a ¼-inch dowel. Cut and drill pieces as shown in the diagram. Slip a 17¼-inch-long dowel through a hole drilled in each 1 by 1. Glue a 1-inch-long piece of 1 by 1 on top of the dowel to form a peak and two more pieces beneath the tips of the "branch" second from the bottom. Bevel the ends of the bottom branch so it will fold easily inside these support blocks.

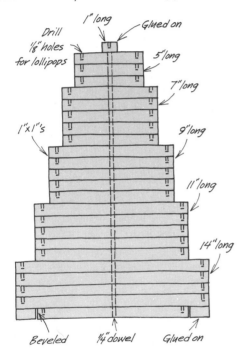

LOLLIPOPS ARE NICE, but you could also adapt this idea to make a tree to hold candy canes, candles, candied apples, or any other taste treat your child likes.

Birthday Cake Animals

This birthday girl has her favorite animals parading around her cake with candles in their backs. Her mother made the animals out of plastic modeling material that hardens when baked in the oven. The material is available in some art supply and toy stores. Any modeling material that hardens could be used instead.

First, shape the animal bodies, then stick toothpicks into them for legs, tails, and beaks. Make a small hole in the animal's back to hold the candle. Bake the animals in the oven according to the instructions on the package of the modeling material. (Do not bake the clay at the same time you bake the cake.) Decorate the finished animals with paint or food dye.

WILL SHE blow out all the candles in one breath? Maybe, maybe not, but she will have the animals to play with later. They are made out of oven-hardened modeling clay.

Candy House

An old-fashioned candy house, built with cardboard boxes, can delight children. You'll need an 18-inch-square piece of plywood for the base and five small, different-sized cardboard boxes.

Stack the boxes on the plywood base so you'll have three roof levels, with the largest box as the central part. Tape the boxes together and secure the whole structure to the base with tape.

Cut roofs of heavy cardboard, allowing 1-inch overhang; bend in half. To attach roofs securely, make two or three 1-inch cuts with a knife through the roofs on each side, just above where the walls will meet them. Set roofs in place. Slide a table knife up through each cut; stick masking tape to knife end. Pull knife back; peel off tape end and stick it to the wall. Press the other end of the tape to the roof.

Frost the house as you would a cake; decorate with hard candy pressed firmly into frosting. *Frosting recipe:* Beat 2 egg whites until stiff. Add 1/2 teaspoon cream of tartar and 1 pound confectioner's sugar. Beat until frosting is stiff enough to hold its peak.

PEPPERMINT STEPS, gum drop edges, sugared fruit windows, and candy cane trim tempt this young kibitzer.

Easter Egg Dyeing

Decorated eggs are as necessary at Easter as a stocking is at Christmas or a cake at a birthday party. In this egg-dyeing technique, you block out the design you want on the egg with masking tape, then dip the egg in dye.

Use hardboiled eggs or, if you plan to keep them, use blown eggs. To blow an egg, prick a hole in each end, making one hole slightly larger than the other. Break the yoke with a needle, then blow the egg through the larger hole into a bowl. Rinse the egg shell out with clear water. Before applying the design and dyeing hardboiled eggs, bring them to room temperature. Handle the eggs as little as possible to avoid getting oil from your hands on them—the oil may resist the dye.

Stick the designs cut from masking tape (stars, squares, hearts, half moons) firmly onto the egg, using your fingernail to smooth and press the edges down. After dipping the egg in Easter egg dye or food coloring, blot it dry and remove the tape.

MASKING TAPE was used in a batiklike technique to decorate eggs.

Gift Wrapping

Why not make a gift's wrapping be as exciting as what's inside? Even a potato-salad carton holding homemade cookies or candy is a present worth putting under the tree or opening at a birthday when decorated like the packages shown here.

With felt pens, glue, yarn, ribbons, and colorful scraps of paper and fabric, you can make a gift wrapping unique, exciting, and mysterious. Odd-shaped cartons and tubes are especially mysterious for a child. Square and rectangular gift boxes take on special interest when you turn them into people or animals or give a hint as to their contents with pasted-on decorations and additions.

ALL YOU NEED to perk up a gift are colorful paper, ribbons, paint or crayons, scraps of fabric, and imagination.

SEE INSTRUCTIONS ON FACING PAGE

A Potpourri of Toys

Friendly Rocking Animals

These simple rocking beasts made from wood and other natural materials create as much excitement for a child as a sophisticated mechanical toy. The construction method for all the animals is a simple gluing and doweling process, requiring little experience and few tools. A ¼-inch drill and a band or saber saw are helpful power tools if you have them. The wood used is vertical grain Douglas fir.

The bodies are basically the same for all the animals— two 1½-inch-thick end pieces joined to 1 by 2s with ⅜-inch dowels, as shown in the photographs. The size of the end pieces varies with the size of the animal. (See drawings on page 86 for measurements.) The giraffe's body is slightly different from the other animals' bodies because circular pieces form the ends and 18-inch-long 2 by 2s are the legs.

(Continued on page 86)

LONG-NECKED GIRAFFE (above) has 2 by 2 legs doweled to 7½-inch circles of fir. Other animals (left and facing page) are made as shown in drawings on page 86. Elephant's ears are leather. Two mops nailed to the lion's head make a mane. Rope creates animals' tails. Dowels and door pulls, glued and screwed in place, make eyes and giraffe's horns. Drawings on page 86 show construction of each animal's head.

Rocking Animals (cont.)

Starting in the middle of the animal's back, join the ends of the 1 by 2s to the end sections by drilling 3/8-inch holes through the 1 by 2s and the edges of the end sections. Apply liberal amounts of plastic resin glue and pound 2-inch-long dowels into the holes. Keep the end pieces parallel to each other and perpendicular to the 1 by 2s while working around the animal's back.

The lion's head is cut from a 4 by 6 (see drawing). For eyes, fasten wooden drawer pulls with dowels. Two floor mops attached with nails make the mane.

The giraffe's head, also cut from a 4 by 6 block, perches atop a 3-foot-long 2 by 4 neck. The ears, made from a piece of leather, are held in a slot between the neck and head. Each 18-inch-long, 2 by 2 leg is joined to a rocker with two dowels and to a body end piece with two more dowels.

The elephant's head looks more complicated than it really is. It consists simply of a series of 4 by 6 blocks—cut as shown in the drawing. The trunk is made from seven 2-inch-thick blocks cut from a 4 by 4 tapered down with a wood rasp and saw. Drill two holes through each block for stringing onto ropes with knots between the blocks.

Attach the animal's neck to his body with plastic resin glue and dowels, driving the dowels (two or three) through holes in the front body section and into corresponding holes in the neck from the inside of the body.

Splintering is a major drawback of Douglas fir, so be sure to round all corners and do a thorough sanding job. The animals can be painted, oiled, or left natural.

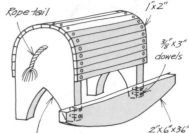

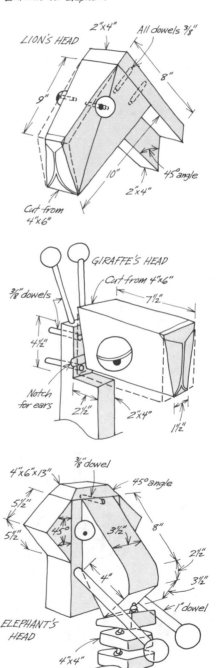

DOWELS hold 1 by 2s to body end pieces. Lengths of 1 by 2s vary: 22" for elephant; 18" for lion; 16" for giraffe.

Two Hobby Horses

Hobby horses are for every child: young rodeo riders, cowboys, highwaymen, and Knights of the Round Table. Here are an old-fashioned broomstick horse and a horse on wheels, both designed for small children.

To make the broomstick horse, stuff the foot of a heavy sock solidly with cotton. Cut round triangles of leather or felt for ears and sew them in place. Sew on buttons or pieces of leather for eyes and stitch a mouth with embroidery thread. Cut a quantity of 4-inch lengths of yarn for the forelock and mane, stitching them through the middle of sock and down neck.

Fashion the bridle from strips of leather, allowing enough extra length for the reins. Cut a broomstick or dowel to a suitable length for the height of the future master. Work the cut end well up into the sock and pack firmly with cotton. Tuck the top of the sock under and tie it tightly around the stick with strong thread. Secure the head by driving upholstery tacks through the end of the sock into the stick.

The horse on wheels has a frame made from a sturdy sawhorse. The front wheels are large casters for maneuverability; the rear wheels are ³/₄-inch plywood disks that rotate on a 1-inch dowel axle fixed in holes drilled at an angle through the legs. Small ¹/₄-inch plywood disks, glued and screwed to the ends of the dowels, hold the wheels on.

The ears are leather triangles, glued and nailed to the ³/₄-inch plywood head. The tail is a length of rope, glued and nailed into a ¹/₂-inch slot in the upright 2 by 4. All other parts are attached with white glue and nails. See drawing for construction details.

MADE FROM A BROOMSTICK and sock, this old-fashioned stick horse is a toy that you yourself might have had as a child.

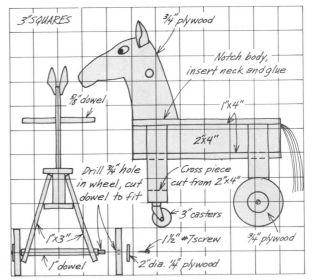

BENIGN LOOKING CRITTER (left) is just right for small children. He can be walked along as the child rides. Follow the drawing above for cutting and assembling the horse.

From Cardboard to City

This child-sized city might require your child's architectural assistance. Or you could elect yourself construction superintendent and turn the project over to young engineering talent for finishing touches.

The city is built from cardboard cartons and boxes, available from most stores. First, the children draw their ideas for windows and doors directly onto the boxes, then you cut them out with a mat or craft knife. Then the buildings are given back to the children, who brush on thinned white glue and cover the boxes with colored paper or color them with poster paint.

Most paper or cardboard boxes can be used for the buildings, but those from department stores are usually thinner and easier to cut. The various gables, chimneys, bays, porticos, and steeples can be created from almost any type of cardboard container—try shoe boxes, paper towel cylinders, and egg cartons. Let the children decorate the additions and attach them to the buildings with tape and glue.

AN ENTIRE VILLAGE (below) was made out of cardboard by children with a little adult help. Child draws on doors and windows; you cut them out. Paint and tissue paper give buildings color. Add-ons such as steeple (above) are cardboard.

IT REALLY WORKS! This miniature greenhouse (above left and right), made according to the drawing below, is a place where children can start and grow small plants and seeds even during the cold season. It fits over an 11 by 16-inch plastic or aluminum kitchen pan on which the potted plants sit. Use weatherproof plastic sheeting for glazing.

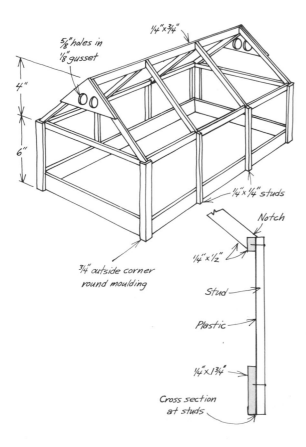

Miniature Greenhouse

Small green thumbs will enjoy growing small plants and seeds in this miniature greenhouse. Start with a low rectangular plastic or aluminum kitchen pan, then construct the greenhouse around it. The pan used in this greenhouse is 11 by 16 inches, the greenhouse 11½ by 16½ inches (inside measurements). If the pan you use is a different size, adjust the measurements of the greenhouse in the drawing accordingly.

First assemble the two long sides, using white glue and small finishing nails. Let the glue dry, then attach the two end sections of the frame and finally erect the roof. Don't attach the two gussets at the end of the gables, the two studs on each side, and the four corner moldings until you've covered the frame with plastic glazing. For glazing, a waterproof clear-plastic sheeting (available at hardware and art supply stores) is best. Cut glazing for the two long sides in single pieces. Attach the plastic with white glue and staples. Cover the staples and joints of the plastic with colored cloth adhesive tape, then nail the gussets, studs, and corner moldings in place. Cut holes in the plastic behind the two finger and ventilation holes in each gusset.

Some plants to try in the greenhouse are miniature ferns and palms, dwarf tomatoes and marigolds, the Venus fly trap, and pitcher plant. Flower and vegetable seeds can also be started. Use peat moss pots and any good planting mix to start the seeds. Place the mix in the pots, wet it, and poke the seeds just under the surface. Keep the greenhouse in any warm spot in the house. When the seedlings are an inch or two high, put it near a sunny window for part of each day. Keep the soil moist. If condensation is excessive when the greenhouse is in the sun, reduce the amount of watering.

Terrariums

Frogs, tadpoles, turtles, lizards, and snakes — the list of creatures that children find and want to bring home seems endless. Since you probably won't want to share your living room with these animals, providing them with their own home is a must. To make a good home for a wild pet, consider his natural environment and then try to duplicate it in miniature. Use a glass aquarium (sold in pet and fish stores) for the three terrariums described below.

A *DESERT TERRARIUM* (for lizards, horned toads, snakes) is the easiest pet home to establish and maintain. Cover the bottom of an aquarium or other pet home with several inches of sand and add rocks for sunning and shade. (Desert animals need the warmth and light of an electric light, but they also need a shady place like a rock cave.) Keep a small dish or jar lid of water in one corner. Add a bare branch, cactus, or other desert plant.

A *WOODLAND TERRARIUM* (chameleons, frogs, salamanders, snakes, toads) should have several plants. Cover the bottom of an aquarium an inch deep with a mixture of coarse gravel and aquarium filter charcoal. Cover this with 2 inches of potting mix. You can use mosses, ferns, liverworts, lichens, or any small moisture-loving plant. Overhead light from an aquarium hood is essential for plants and pet. (Be sure the entire top is covered to prevent escapes.) Since there is no drainage, soil should be kept barely damp. Sink a dish of water into the soil (see drawing) for drinking and cooling off.

An *AQUA-TERRARIUM* (frogs, tadpoles, newts, turtles) combines water and dry land. The idea is to provide swimming room as well as a place to crawl out and sun. The aqua-terrarium in the drawing is made by cutting a piece of glass the width of the aquarium and long enough so that when you place it at a 45° angle, the top edge is at least 4 inches from the bottom. Use a silicone rubber sealer to make a watertight seal. Fill one side with water; fill the other side with soil, using the same method discussed for the woodland terrarium, and then add plants. It's important to keep the water clean; change it frequently. An under-gravel aquarium filter will help, but you still must change the water occasionally.

GOPHER SNAKE could live in a wooden box with sliding glass front and screened vents, as below, or in a glass terrarium.

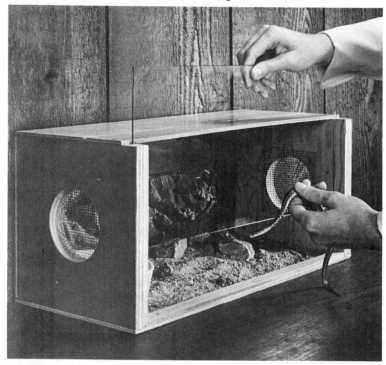

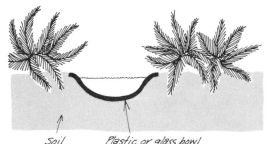

Soil   Plastic or glass bowl

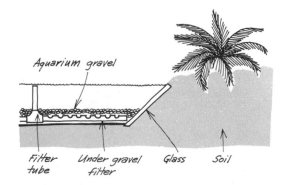

Aquarium gravel

Filter tube   Under gravel filter   Glass   Soil

WOODLAND TERRARIUM (top) should be heavily planted. Aqua-terrarium (below) provides land and swimming areas.

GLASS TERRARIUMS make good homes for wild creatures that children often bring home. This turtle pleasantly swims in his aqua-terrarium. Always try to recreate the animal's native environment.

The most common reptile and amphibian pets are listed below. Information on care for each includes food and environment. Where temperatures stated are higher than room temperature, pets can be kept warm by placing an aquarium heater-thermostat in a jar of water and setting it in one corner of the terrarium. Reptiles and amphibians are cold-blooded; this means they will be active and hungry at warm temperatures and lethargic when it's cool.

Remember that not all wild creatures thrive in captivity. If a pet goes into a decline, better release him. Many people prefer to observe a wild pet for only a few weeks and then let it go. This is probably the most humane policy if the child's interest flags.

• Anolis (sold as chameleons). Require a good deal of care; woodland terrarium; 70° to 80°. Sprinkle or mist spray the terrarium daily. Chameleons eat live flies and mealworms.

• Frogs. Woodland or aqua-terrarium, according to the frog's natural habitat. Keep moist and between 60° and 70°. Feed frogs lean meat, pellet turtle food. Keep top covered.

• Salamanders. Woodland terrarium; 60° to 70°; keep moist. Feed salamanders mealworms, earthworms, small insects. Salamanders often like to hide during the day.

• Snakes. Desert or woodland terrarium; 65° and above. Most prefer a warm, dry environment. Feed snakes small live animals such as mice and large insects. Force feeding is not advised. Provide snakes with a dish of water and a hiding place such as a rock cave.

• Tadpoles. Aqua-terrarium, same conditions as frogs. Tadpoles eat vegetable matter, such as fine-leafed water plants. Provide rocks or land for them to crawl onto when they change into frogs or toads.

• Toads. Woodland terrarium; 60° to 70°; keep moist. Toads eat mealworms, earthworms, insects; food must move. Many toads will bury themselves for periods of time.

• Water turtles. Aqua-terrarium. Turtles eat fresh lean meat (earthworms are a treat), water plants. Turtles must be fed in the water. Provide overhead light and a rock for basking.

The Busy Cloth

Here is a "busy cloth." Its young owner can lace, button, buckle, and snap various pockets and openings; she can take the cloth along on car trips; store toys inside of it; roll it up for an overnight visit to a friend's house. In making a busy cloth, you can vary the pockets, snaps, and buckles, changing their sizes or using different materials.

The busy cloth shown here was made from 2½ yards of 45-inch permanent press fabric; 1½ yards of various contrasting 45-inch fabrics for pockets, beak, buttons, and straps; ¼ yard of heavy nylon net; ⅔ yard (18 inches wide) of iron-on stiffening fabric; an 11 by 20-inch piece of washable pile; two 22-inch neckline type zippers; 14 large grommets; 2½ yards of cotton cording; a covered-buckle kit; a hook-type buckle and slide; and two 10-inch strips of snap tape. Facing fabric is optional.

To make the main part of the busy cloth, cut the 2½ yards of 45-inch permanent press fabric in half. One piece is for all pocket details; the other is for the backing. On the wrong side of one of the fabric halves, draw two 23-inch-long chalk lines centered on the cloth and 18 inches from the cut edges (not the selvages) to use as a guide for positioning the zippers. Follow the directions on the zipper package and sew one of the zippers into the cloth along the chalk line near the bird-face pocket. (Note right side of cloth in the photograph.)

To make the see-through pocket, cut a piece of one of the contrasting fabrics 13 inches wide and 22 inches long and cut windows into it. Window size is optional; those in this busy cloth are 7½ inches square. Make a ¼-inch diagonal slash in each corner of the windows, then fold the window edges under to create a ¼-inch seam allowance. Pin three thicknesses of nylon net (9 by 20 inches each) onto the underside of the fabric and machine stitch along all edges. Stitch an edge of the window pocket to one side of the second zipper onto the cloth along the chalk line. Finally, sew the pocket edges onto the cloth.

For the lacing section, cut the iron-on facing to 8½ by 24 inches and apply it to the wrong side of the center section of the cloth. Insert two rows (4 inches apart) of 5 grommets each in

LEARNING TO BUTTON, lace, snap, and buckle is fun on the busy cloth. Pockets open differently: bird pocket (right) buttons and snaps; zippers and lacing in center.

the cloth according to the package directions. Use cotton cord for the lacing; wrap the ends of the cord with thread to prevent raveling.

The bird-face pocket is made from a piece of contrasting fabric 11 inches wide and 23 inches long. Fold the material in half, right side out, then press. Use the crease as a guide for sewing the beak to the upper side and snap tape to the underside of the pocket. Separate the snap tape and stitch the 10-inch strips to the pockets about ¾ inch from each side edge.

Cut the beak out of contrasting fabric and sew it onto the pocket. A piece of 11 by 20-inch pile fabric is used for the flap. Fold the fabric in half, right sides together, stitch the edges together, and turn right side out. Put two button holes about 3½ inches apart in the flap. Sew to the top (back) edges of the pocket. Hem the raw edges of the pocket. To complete, place right sides together, stitch side edges of the pocket, turn right side out, and press. Check the placement of the pocket on the cloth and stitch corresponding 10-inch strips of snap tape to the cloth. Cover the buttons and sew them into place on the pocket section of the material.

All of the straps are 4 inches wide and made from contrasting fabric. Cut a 16-inch-long strip for the strap with the buckle and a 10-inch strip for the strap with grommets. Fold the strips lengthwise down the center (right sides together) and stitch. Turn the strips right side out and press. Attach the buckles to the ends of the straps. To attach the straps to the cloth, fold each in half with the right sides together, then pin or baste the fold in each to the right side of the cloth and 14 inches in from each corner. (Straps should be pointing inwards towards center of the cloth.)

With all of the attachments and pockets on the cloth, you're ready to sew on the backing. Place the cloth and cloth backing right sides together. Match the selvages and then trim the edges. Stitch all of the sides together and turn the cloth right side out through the zipper opening. To form the pocket for the first zipper opening (under the bird-face pocket), draw chalk lines (13 and 22 inches) around the pocket and stitch through both layers of cloth; leave the lacing side open so the child can reach underneath.

PULLOFF BIRDFACE POCKET has oversize buttons and snap tape that small hands like to open and close.

SEE-THROUGH NET WINDOWS sewn onto the cloth leave no guessing about contents. Open and close with zipper.

Do-anything Machine

The do-anything machine comes about as close as possible to doing and being anything you and your children want. It is a whimsical collection of more than 20 gadgets to pull, push, swing, crank, and turn with accompanying moos, ding-a-lings, beep-beeps, and other sounds. It has things to open and close and holes to peer into and drop things down, and you could add or incorporate just about any of your own ideas.

The basic design of the do-anything machine is a box of ½-inch plywood, 3 feet square and 18 inches high, supported on 1½-inch wood dowel legs with casters. The top of the box is 27 inches off the ground.

No two do-anything machines will be outfitted in the same way. The photograph and drawings of this one might suggest ideas that you could incorporate into a do-anything machine of your own.

IT COULD BE ANYTHING. Attachments and accessories on an anything machine depend on what you have or find.

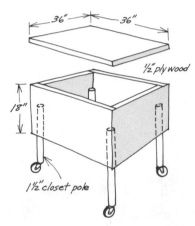

CONSTRUCTION IS SIMPLE and straightforward. To keep small hands from inner machinery, add a bottom.

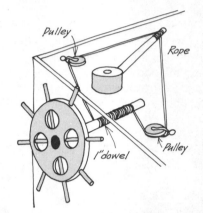

STEERING WHEEL could operate any sort of mechanism or toy, such as a boom, rudder, toy car, or boat.

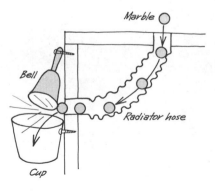

RIBBED RADIATOR HOSE inside the box leads marble, dropped through hole, out the side where it hits a bell.

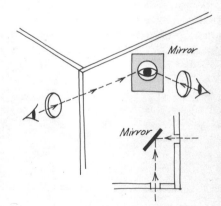

AROUND THE CORNER SPYING is allowed by a small mirror inside the box and peepholes drilled in the sides.

A Metallophone is a Musical Instrument

For children who like to make noise, here is the metallophone. Its bars are tubes of 3/4-inch steel electrical conduit, sold at hardware and electrical stores or, since you only need short pieces, perhaps available from electrical contractors as scrap. If you tune the metallophone against a piano, it will have a surprisingly melodious tone. The base is a 2 by 3-foot piece of 1/8-inch lauan plywood, cut as shown in the drawing. The tubes lie on two 1 by 2 by 36-inch strips of polyurethane foam that are glued to the base.

The polyurethane should be soft (often called 10 percent) foam, so the tubes can vibrate easily when struck by the wooden mallets. Use a serrated knife to cut notches in both strips about 1 3/4 inches apart; these notches position and hold the tubes.

The tone of each tube depends on its length (as well as on the particular piece of electrical conduit, since conduit varies somewhat in thickness) so tuning is a matter of trial and error. You'll doubtless get some sour notes at first, but by cutting or grinding down the length of the tube or, when necessary, substituting a longer tube, you will soon have a xylophonelike musical instrument.

To find C above middle C, start with a tube about 14 inches long; for high C, try a tube about 9 7/8 inches long. Each of the six tubes in between is about 1/2 inch longer than the next higher one. Down the scale, the tubes increase about 3/4 inch in length.

The metallophone shown here has 18 tubes. The shortest is about 8 inches, the longest about 20 inches. The mallets are two 1 1/2-inch round hardwood drawer knobs glued to lengths of 1/4-inch wood dowels that serve as handles.

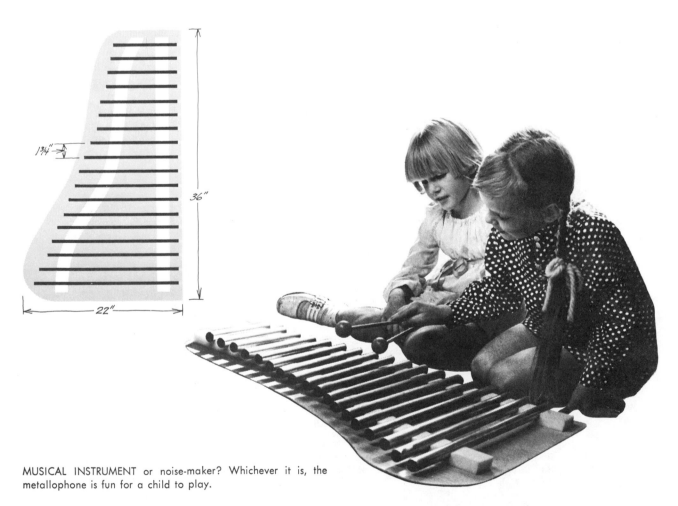

MUSICAL INSTRUMENT or noise-maker? Whichever it is, the metallophone is fun for a child to play.

Index

Alligator puppet, 40-41
Animal toys
  wooden, 6, 10-12
  cloth, 27-32
Apron, 37

Barrel exerciser, 51
Basketball backstop, 53
Bathtub toy, 12
Bean bags, 30
Bear spread, 35
Beds, 68-69
Big jaw puppets, 40-41
Blackboards, 67
Boats, wooden, 6
Bookshelf doll house, 18-19
Building blocks, 9
Building toys, 8, 9, 56, 57
Bulletin boards, 67
Busy cloth, 92-93

Cam critters, 6
Candy house, 82
Cardboard city, 88
Cardboard playhouse, 58-59
Catapult, 9
Cars, wooden, 5
Christmas stockings, 33
Climbing structure, 48
Cloth toys, 26-37
Cork toy, 12
Costumes, 74-77
Counting toy, 13
Craft table, 72-73

Do-anything machine, 94
Doll house furniture, 25
Doll houses, 16-24
Doll house-trailer, 21
Dolls, stuffed, 27
Drawing table, 15

Easter eggs, 82

Felt chickens, 32
Felt turtle, 66
Four story doll house, 16
Frog puppet, 40-41
Furniture, 66-73

Gift wrapping, 83
Giraffe, rocking, 55
Greenhouse, miniature, 89

Halloween, 74-77
Hillside doll house, 20
Hobby horses, 87

Igloo playhouse, 58

Jigsaw puzzle, 13
Jump rope handles, 33

Kites, 54

Lambs, 12
Locomotive, 56
Lounge, 70

Mailing tube train, 14
Marionettes, 38-39
Masks, 77
Metallophone, 95
Mobile, 66
Monkeys, 29

Nesting toy, 32

Outdoor building toys, 56, 57
Owls, 31

Paint smock, 36
Paper bag costumes, 76
Party games, 78-79
Party ideas, 78-81
Patchwork dog, 31
Pillows, 34
Piñata party, 80
Ping pong table, 72
Play cubes, 69
Playhouse bed, 68
Playhouses, 58-63
Play yard equipment, 46-62
Play yard ideas, 46-50
Play yard structure, 46-47
Plywood building toy, 57
Plywood zoo, 8
Pop puppet, 44
Portable playhouse, 60
Pull toys, 6, 7, 10, 11
Puppets, 38-44
Puppet theater, 45
Puzzle, 13

Rag dolls, 27
Reach-into doll house, 24
Revolving doll house, 22-23
Rocking animals, 55, 84-86

Sand boxes, 50
Sewing projects, 26-37
Slide, 52
Smock, 36
Sock monkeys, 29
Sock puppets, 42-43
Stuffed animals, 27-31
Swimming pool basketball, 53
Swing, 49

Table for crafts, 72
Tent playhouse, 60
Terrariums, 90-91
Theatrical make up, 74-75
Toy box, 15
Toys on wheels, 5-7, 9-11
Train, toy, 14
Train, headboard, 69
Triangle building toy, 56

Wall decorations, 65-67
Wiggling beasts, 10-11
Wobble toys, 7
Wooden toys, 4-15

Xylophone, 95

Yarn animals, 28